First World War
and Army of Occupation
War Diary
France, Belgium and Germany

32 DIVISION
Divisional Troops
155 Brigade Royal Field Artillery
29 December 1915 - 27 February 1917

WO95/2380/3

The Naval & Military Press Ltd
www.nmarchive.com
Published in association with The National Archives

Published by

The Naval & Military Press Ltd

Unit 10 Ridgewood Industrial Park,

Uckfield, East Sussex,

TN22 5QE England

Tel: +44 (0) 1825 749494

www.naval-military-press.com

www.nmarchive.com

This diary has been reprinted in facsimile from the original. Any imperfections are inevitably reproduced and the quality may fall short of modern type and cartographic standards.

© **Crown Copyright**
Images reproduced by permission of The National Archives, London, England, 2015.

Contents

Document type	Place/Title	Date From	Date To
Heading	WO95/2380-3		
Heading	32nd Divisional Divl Artillery 155th Bde. R.F.A. Jan 1916-Feb 1917 To 1 Army		
Heading	32nd Divisional Artillery 155 Brigade R.F.A. January 1916 Feb 1917		
War Diary	Southampton	29/12/1915	29/12/1915
War Diary	La Havre	01/01/1916	04/01/1916
War Diary	Argoeuves	05/01/1916	05/01/1916
War Diary	Frechencourt	05/01/1916	05/01/1916
War Diary	Martinsart	06/01/1916	31/01/1916
Miscellaneous	Brigade Orders.	10/02/1916	10/02/1916
Heading	32nd Divisional Artillery 155th Brigade R.F.A. February 1916		
War Diary	Courcelles	03/02/1916	03/02/1916
War Diary	Martinsart	01/02/1916	14/02/1916
War Diary	Frechencourt	14/02/1916	14/02/1916
War Diary	Martinsart	15/02/1916	15/02/1916
War Diary	Frechencourt And Montigny		
War Diary	Montigny	16/02/1916	29/02/1916
Heading	32nd Divisional Artillery. 155th Brigade R.F.A. March 1916		
War Diary	Montigny	01/03/1916	02/03/1916
War Diary	Albert	02/03/1916	07/04/1916
War Diary	Rubempre	08/04/1916	13/04/1916
War Diary	Contay	14/04/1916	30/04/1916
Heading	32nd Divisional Artillery. 155th Brigade R.F.A. May 1916		
War Diary	Contay	01/05/1916	31/05/1916
Heading	32nd Divisional Artillery. 155th Brigade Royal Field Artillery June 1916		
War Diary	Contay	08/06/1916	11/06/1916
War Diary	Bouzincourt	13/06/1916	26/06/1916
War Diary	Bluff	27/06/1916	27/06/1916
War Diary	Authville	28/06/1916	28/06/1916
War Diary	Bluff	29/06/1916	29/06/1916
War Diary	Authville	29/06/1916	30/06/1916
Heading	War Diary Headquarters 155th Brigade R.F.A. (32nd Division) July 1916		
War Diary	Authville	01/07/1916	07/07/1916
War Diary	Warloy	08/07/1916	18/07/1916
War Diary	Milly	19/07/1916	19/07/1916
War Diary	Monchel	20/07/1916	20/07/1916
War Diary	Wavrans	21/07/1916	21/07/1916
War Diary	Ames	22/07/1916	28/07/1916
War Diary	Marles Les Mines	29/07/1916	31/07/1916
Heading	32nd Divisional Artillery.155th Brigade R.F.A. August 1916		
War Diary	Merle Les Mines	01/08/1916	03/08/1916
War Diary	Annequin	04/08/1916	09/08/1916
War Diary	Le Preol	10/08/1916	31/08/1916

Heading	32nd Divisional Artillery. 155th Brigade R.F.A. September 1916		
War Diary	Le Preol	01/09/1916	30/09/1916
Heading	32nd Divisional Artillery. 155th Brigade R.F.A. October 1916		
War Diary	Le Preol	05/10/1916	15/10/1916
War Diary	Lapugnoy	16/10/1916	17/10/1916
War Diary	Rebreuvette	18/10/1916	18/10/1916
War Diary	Authieule	19/10/1916	19/10/1916
War Diary	Mailly Mailley	20/10/1916	31/10/1916
Heading	32nd Divisional Artillery. 155th Brigade R.F.A. November 1916		
War Diary	Mailly-Maillet	03/11/1916	30/11/1916
Heading	32nd Divisional Artillery 155th Brigade R.F.A. December 1916		
War Diary	Louvencourt	04/12/1916	04/12/1916
War Diary	St Leger	06/12/1916	31/12/1916
Heading	War Diary 155th Brigade R.F.A. Vol No. 90th 95 January 1st To January 31st 1917		
War Diary	Authieule	02/01/1917	02/01/1917
War Diary	Mailly Maillet	03/01/1917	16/01/1917
War Diary	Courcelles	17/01/1917	31/01/1917
Heading	War Diary 155th (Army) FA Bde Vol XV (No 96 To 99) February 1st To February 28th 1917		
War Diary	Courcelles	04/02/1917	27/02/1917
Operation(al) Order(s)	Right Artillery Group Operation Order No. 3		
Miscellaneous	Appendix "A"		
Miscellaneous	Ammendment To Right Artillery Group O.O. No. 3	14/02/1917	14/02/1917
Miscellaneous	Right Artillery Group Operation Order No. 4	27/02/1917	27/02/1917

32ND DIVISION
DIVL ARTILLERY

155TH BDE R.F.A.
JAN 1916-FEB 1917

TO I ARMY

32ND DIVISION
DIVL ARTILLERY

32nd Divisional Artillery.

155th BRIGADE R. F. A.

JANUARY 1 9 1 6

Feb 1917

WAR DIARY
or
INTELLIGENCE SUMMARY.
(Erase heading not required.)

Army Form C. 2118.

Place	Date	Hour	Summary of Events and Information	Remarks and references to Appendices

Southampton	1915. Dec 29.	6.0 a.m. 9 p.m.	The 155th Brigade R.F.A. left Forest Hills on 29th December 1915 for Southampton. Entrainment was completed during the evening of the day. Arrived Le Havre early morning 30th and 31st December – A Battery and Brigade Remts. Col. arrives morning of 30th and proceeded to other Ranks Camp, Le Havre. The B.C. and D and Headquarter Staff arriving 31st proceeds to No 2 Camp at Sanvic, Le Havre. The following are details of Personnel and equipment of the Brigade on arrival at Le Havre :–
			
			Headquarters Staff.
			Officer Commanding Lieut-Col R.F.P. Bunbury R.F.A.
			Adjutant Capt. H.E. Barker R.F.A.
			Orderly Officer 2nd Lieut. R.D. Dunnell R.F.A.
			Medical Officer Lieut. N.B. Taylor R.A.M.C.
			Veterinary Officer Lieut. F.J. Smith A.V.C.
			Signal Officer 2nd Lieut. Nicholson R.F.A.
			                                        2nd Lieut. E. Pool Jones R.F.A.
			                                        2nd Lieut. J.H. Wybury R.F.A.
			                                        2nd Lieut. A. Nicholls R.F.A.
			
			A Battery Acting Bty Comdt Field	

WAR DIARY
or
INTELLIGENCE SUMMARY.
(Erase heading not required.)

Place	Date	Hour	Summary of Events and Information	Remarks and references to Appendices
			B. Battery. Battery Commander – Captain H.P. Preest-Jones R.H.A. Lieut. R. Mayer R.H.A. 2nd Lieut. Sidney Seed R.H.A. 2nd Lieut. Harold Shoutz R.H.A.	
			C. Battery. Battery Commander – Captain P.B. Wharton R.H.A. Lieut. Cp. Leaky R.H.A. 2Lt. A.S. Mercer R.H.A. 2Lt. C.M. Manuel R.H.A.	
			D. Battery. Battery Commander – Captain H.V.R. Butler R.H.A. Lieut. H.D. Wilkinson R.H.A. 2Lieut. E. Sugden R.H.A. Lieut. Chalshaw Hare R.H.A.	

WAR DIARY
or
INTELLIGENCE SUMMARY.
(Erase heading not required.)

Army Form C. 2118.

Place	Date	Hour	Summary of Events and Information	Remarks and references to Appendices

Brigade Ammunition Column
Commander - acting -   Lieut. C.J. Manson, R.A.
                        2nd Lieut. G.J. Prinsloo, R.A.
                        2nd Lieut. E.B. Battersby, R.A.

Total Officers 24, Other ranks 728, Horses 729, Issues 16, Luchr wagons 56, G.S. wagons 9, Carts 11,
Ammunition brought from England –
18 Pdr. Shrapnel, 1216 rnds Bde. Park Colm, 2816 rnds Batteries, total 4032.
" " " B.P.&L. Colm, 424,000 rnds, totalling 27/110 ” " 451/110.
Small Arms Rnds,

| Le Havre | 7.1.am 6 a.m. | A. Bty. and Park Colm entrained for Amiens – Hdqrs. Staff and B.C. + D. Btries entrained on Sunday morning for Amiens. On arrival there proceeded by road to ARGOEUVRES. The Brigade was billeted until 5th inst. 2.& 1. Nichols reported Capt. and of kinds to Brigade. The Brigade left at 8 a.m. for Freshencourt arriving at 9.30 a.m. Here the Bde. was billeted until next morning, Thursday, 6 th Jan. The General & Battery | |
| ARGOEUVRES | 2nd 5.8 a.m. | | | |

WAR DIARY
or
INTELLIGENCE SUMMARY.

Place	Date	Hour	Summary of Events and Information	Remarks and references to Appendices
FRECHENCOURT	1916. Jan 5.	8 a.m.	Guns moved off at 8 a.m. for MARTINSART with half sections of Batteries following.	
MARTINSART	Jan 6.	6.30 pm	Arrived at MARTINSART. the Officer Commanding met OC. 2nd Highland F.A. Brigade whom he relieved. Half section Batteries were placed in position half	
do.	Jan 7	3 pm	Section of 2nd Highland F.A. Bde. having vacated OC. Guns ** the other half sections of guns were brought up to the firing line and placed in position. Registrations were begun on Jan 7th. On commencing into action the Officer Commanding was appointed Officer Commanding Left-Group of 32nd Divisional Artillery. The Batteries positions taken up were as follows :-	
			1 (A)/155 Battery — Regt. "Orillers" — 57 D. Lt. — Harrison (Saxony) — M.B. 30.95 (near MARTINSART.)	
			B/155 " " " — Beaumont — 57 D. b — 1 and 2 — Q. 34. b. 5. (near MESNIL)	
			C/155 " " — do — — do — Q. 34. b. 3. (near MESNIL)	
			D/155 " " — Orillers — 57 D. 8 F — 4 — " — h. 18. a. 15. 80 (near AVELUY)	
			The Zone covered by the Brigade extended from the line BEAUCOURT-SUR-ANCRE to MARTINSART and the line 500 yds. South of AUTHUILLE to MARTINSART. Round Zires 24 hours to 6 a.m. 8th — 86 English.	
do.	Jan 8.	10 a.m.	Aeroplane Louis over B. By. Lt. Lewis machine. Bylow By. used to left Group.	
		3.20 pm	Heavy firing into MESNIK. Rounds fired 15th to 6 a.m. 9th.	

WAR DIARY
or
INTELLIGENCE SUMMARY.
(Erase heading not required.)

Place	Date	Hour	Summary of Events and Information	Remarks and references to Appendices
MARTINSART	1916 Jan. 9		Quiet day. Occasional shelling into trenches. Weather - fair. Registration proceeding. Shells fired by Bde - 24 Lno.t 6 g.m 9 am - 93 " " " A'noons Rep. (13/16cwt) - 42/135	
do.	Jan 10		French Batties (Hostile) active into trenches. Frequent Artillery replies called for. Registrations of our Batteries proceeding. Otherwise Quiet. Weather good & clean. B.By. effecting shells on enemy transport passing thro' THIEPVAL. Shells expended 112.	
do.	Jan 11		Enemy French Batties still active. Batteries firing 16 Regists and reply. 15 T.M's very little hostile artillery observed. Flares every few from direction of FERME DU MOUQUET observed. Shells expended 69. Weather clean	
do.	Jan 12		Quiet day. Very little hostile fire. A hostile biplane (VOISIN 74 PE apparently) with French marks flew over from the German lines (entries at 6 Bde) at a height of 3000 feet ovickes over own lines and returned via ST PIERRE DIVION. 2 hostile Observation Balloons up during the day.	[signature]

WAR DIARY
or
INTELLIGENCE SUMMARY.

(Erase heading not required.)

Instructions regarding War Diaries and Intelligence Summaries are contained in F. S. Regs., Part II. and the Staff Manual respectively. Title pages will be prepared in manuscript.

Place	Date	Hour	Summary of Events and Information	Remarks and references to Appendices
MARTINSART.	1916 Jan. 12. (Contd.)	—	Weather clear and fine. Registration of B'des proceeding and rather more than usual Reply from Artillery asked for. Several working parties observed and fired upon with effect. Shells expended 159.	
do.	Jan. 13.	—	Weather clear. Train and Motor Transports observing activity as usual MONT-LE-GRAND. Nearly made French (Hostile) fires upon with HE not with effect. Very little hostile artillery observed. Expended 108 Rounds.	
do	Jan. 14.	—	Hostile artillery more active. Several rounds Shrapnel and HE fired into MARTIN WOOD from N. from direction of BEAUMONT-HAMEL. Considerable movement observed on CRUCIFIX Corner, THIEPVAL. Fired on with effect (presumed ration dump). Trench Mortars active. Weather fine and clear. Shells expended 62.	

WAR DIARY or INTELLIGENCE SUMMARY.

(Erase heading not required.)

Army Form C. 2118.

Instructions regarding War Diaries and Intelligence Summaries are contained in F.S. Regs., Part II. and the Staff Manual respectively. Title pages will be prepared in manuscript.

Hour, Date, Place	Summary of Events and Information	Remarks and references to Appendices
MARTINSART. Jan. 15. 1916.	Enemy artillery quiet – a few rounds only fired into trenches of Extra Gh and G.2. R. Leod shoot given at 10.52 p.m. 15 Btes. to the Brigade – All guns fired within 3½ minutes. No one was present (R. fire given was a counter from the night BARRAGE line.) 1 Shell exploded 112.	
MARTINSART. Jan. 16. 1916.	Enemy shelled MESNIL at various intervals with 77 mm and 10.5 cm. shells – also Trench Pards 148 and 149 – heavy Battering continues Regisbation and field gun Machine Gun emplacement and trench mortars specially. C/Battery opened fire upon T mm when she failed to avoid challenge at Sun Posts PRESENT. We got any Enquiries implicatly but no result. Fok donny at 15 the identity Stella fires 85. 10.p.m	

Army Form C. 2118.

WAR DIARY
or
INTELLIGENCE SUMMARY.
(Erase heading not required.)

Instructions regarding War Diaries and Intelligence Summaries are contained in F.S. Regs., Part II. and the Staff Manual respectively. Title pages will be prepared in manuscript.

Hour, Date, Place	Summary of Events and Information	Remarks and references to Appendices
Jan 17. 1916. 3.15 pm. MARTINSART.	Enemy fires a few salvos on AUTHUILLE during day. Our Batteries replied on THIEPVAL - also on Machine Gun positions with effect.	
10.40 am	Clouds of smoke seen to blow over our Trenches from German lines. No trace of gas reported. Shells expended 66. Weather fair, raining in morning.	
MARTINSART. Jan 18. 1916.	AUTHUILLE again shelled at 12 noon. Trench Mortars again very active and enemy shelled between AVELUY and MESNIL WOODS. We replied on THIEPVAL and Trenches. Weather fair. Shells expended 35.	
Jan 19. 1916.	Heavy enemy shelling into Trenches Points 146 and 149, 157 and 158 and the ground to rear of THIEPVAL WOOD. Bombardment as above by Group Post Hugbes, Fort Fleur. Trenches ¾" Rot 20. 25B. The result was very effective.	

WAR DIARY
or
INTELLIGENCE SUMMARY.

(Erase heading not required.)

Army Form C. 2118.

Instructions regarding War Diaries and Intelligence Summaries are contained in F. S. Regs., Part II. and the Staff Manual respectively. Title pages will be prepared in manuscript.

Hour, Date, Place	Summary of Events and Information	Remarks and references to Appendices
MARTINSART. Jan 19/16. (contd.)	Bursts of the tracks hay from in our front. Weather - Fine and clear. Shells expended, 313.	
MARTINSART. Jan 20/16.	C. Battery shelled new works observed at R.20.C.7.3. - my effect. B.By. position (Q.34.8.4.8) shelled but no damage done. Intermittent shelling by enemy during the day in various parts. Trains observed at ACHIET-LE-GRAND at frequent intervals during the day. Shells expended, 90. Weather - clear.	
MARTINSART. Jan 21/16.	Enemy heavily shelled him also in locality Q.36.D. and N.E. of MESNIL - also THIEPVAL WOOD. We replied on their trenches with effect. Trench Mortars his Machine Guns active. Weather - Fair. Shells expended 71.	

WAR DIARY
or
INTELLIGENCE SUMMARY.

Army Form C. 2118.

(Erase heading not required.)

Hour, Date, Place	Summary of Events and Information	Remarks and references to Appendices
MARTINSART. Jan. 22.	Enemy's Artillery fire distributed over various parts of the line but no serious bombardment. Our Batteries fired at INTERVAL at 4.46 p.m. 5 gtds with Heavy Battery of the 10th Corps at MESNIL, HAMEL, AUTHVILLE, Avelwy. (Weather good, clear) Shells fired, 41.	
Ditto. Jan. 23.	Enemy artillery more active than on 22.D. Fired a number of trench mortar bombs into our Battalion H.Q. R.Co. trenches. Also shelled AUTHVILLE at 4.15 p.m. French Mortar Batas. trenches fair. Shells returned 72. No replies put on gun but not heavily.	
Ditto. Jan. 24.	Weather fair - wind in morning. Enemy trench mortar active - replies to them. Our officers Enemy shelled S.I. Salt trenches PRESLY, & AUTHVILLE. Shells expended 50.	

WAR DIARY
or
INTELLIGENCE SUMMARY.

Army Form C. 2118.

Hour, Date, Place	Summary of Events and Information	Remarks and references to Appendices
MARTINSART. Jan. 25.	Batteries of 151st Bde R.F.A. shelled locality of THIEPVAL and hostile around country (R.25.c). 250 rounds. Observers reported extensive damage done to trenches. Byes (Minny) O.P. also shot in the High Explosive shells. Enemy Battery near TAILLES and another his own bombarded 1 Company E. Yorks. Every attempt to cause Wood & trenches. Enemy shrapnel & .... bursts. Very good. Bul shells opened to say. 347.	
Ditto. Jan. 26.	French Battery bombs from our very active .... section in both on Calos S. Hans G.2 and two Paints and NEWRY ROADS AUTHUILLE and wood at THIEPVAL. The afternoon shells the vicinity of THIEPVAL and trenches. Throughout there was a slight drift. ... went on the vicinity of trenches ANCRE - THIEPVAL with 40 Rounds of shrapnel and 93 Rds of High Explosive. Weather fine throughout the day - clear, ... reports. Weather good. Expended. #172.	

Army Form C. 2118.

WAR DIARY
or
INTELLIGENCE SUMMARY.
(Erase heading not required.)

Instructions regarding War Diaries and Intelligence Summaries are contained in F.S. Regs., Part II. and the Staff Manual respectively. Title pages will be prepared in manuscript.

Hour, Date, Place	Summary of Events and Information	Remarks and references to Appendices
MARTINSART. Jan 27-1916.	Enemy Trench Mortars very active on G.1 Salient but LW. fireings done. PUTHUILLE again shelled but not heavily. Movement of men at POZIERES observed at POZIERES - fired on with success (Time Smoked). Byles (How.) T.B.s effectively dispersed working party at Sells expended 103. Rounds - Fire	
MARTINSART. Jan 28-1916.	Continued activity of Trench Mortars (toitch) in G.1 Sector PUTHUILLE was again heavily shelled at 6p.m - 80/100 shells exploding - very little loss of life. AVELUY & Wood were again shelled at 1st Same time. Sells expended 159	
ditto. Jan 29/16	THIEPVAL WOOD and G.2 Salient heavily shelled at Noon - and HAMEL + AVELUY WOOD Shelled Byles T.B. replies with 32 rounds of shrapnel doing much damage to Trenches at and around THIEPVAL WOOD. Few enemy seen moving in enemy trenches - also near shelters and dugouts but any of activity - No signs of enemy. Several flares observed leaving MARTINPUICH LE GRAND and HAMEL - shells good - Shell. expended 169.	

(73989) W4141—463. 400,000. 9/14. H.&J.Ltd. Forms/C. 2118/10.

WAR DIARY
or
INTELLIGENCE SUMMARY.
(Erase heading not required.)

Army Form C. 2118.

Hour, Date, Place	Summary of Events and Information	Remarks and references to Appendices
MARTINSART. Jan 30/16.	A very quiet day - misty & observation impossible. Shelled 2 batteries by sound - just a few rounds at G.2 Eckhäfringof and hyles to serenade Boom Apost DG. Sur shots reported flat BRAY had scored a plus - Shells reported 4".	
ditto Jan 31/16	Trentin clear. Every battery with very active Day shelled (most heavy) AVELUY and AUTHUILLE again. No damage done. On some distance away looking south with good shoots. J. Sec. Henry firing from reported from Bots shell contined to extend N.N.E. South of ALBERT. Shells reported 5.8.	

Brigade Orders
By Lt Col W St P Bunbury RFA Comdg 155th Bde R.F.A.
10-2-16

1. Strength.
The following having been evacuated from the Divisional Area are struck off the strength of the Brigade from the 8th inst:—

L18785 Dr Stott J.E. — Amm Column
L5670 Dr Clough J. — Bde Staff.

2. DRO's

#58 Civilian Forges
The rate of pay for hire of civilian forges is 1 franc per day without coal and 3 francs per day with coal — to be paid through Billeting Certificate.

#60 Roads — Closing of
The direct road from ALLONVILLE to POULAINVILLE is closed to motor traffic pending repairs.

(462) The road from Laviéville to Bouzincourt is closed for all lorry traffic.

#64 Use of Roads
The following roads will not be used during daylight for the provision of Supplies, R.E. Stores & ammunition, except in cases of extreme urgency:—
The MILLENCOURT — ALBERT Road
The ALBERT — AVELUY Road.

#65 Road Control
During the next three days the SENLIS — HENENCOURT Road will not be used during daylight by any larger party than a Section of Infantry, or a single wagon.

(Sgd) W.J. Barker Capt R
Adjt 155th Bde RFA

32nd Divisional Artillery

155th BRIGADE R. F. A.

FEBRUARY 1 9 1 6

Army Form C. 2118

WAR DIARY
or
INTELLIGENCE SUMMARY
(Erase heading not required.)

No 96

MAP 57D 1/40,000
HEBUTERNE TRENCH MAP 1/10,000

Vol 15

Place	Date	Hour	Summary of Events and Information	Remarks and references to Appendices
COURCELLES	Feb 3		On the night of the 2/3 Feb the 19th Div took over the left subsections front from the 32nd Div as far south as FLAG AVENUE (inclusive). The new 19th Div Artillery Rightgroup was formed under Lt Col. HALLIARD R.S.A.R.F.A. consisting of Hindpreston 155 Bde R.F.A, A B C & D batteries 168 Brigade R.F.A. This group relieved the front taken over from the 32nd Div as where the old 19th Div Arty Rightgroup (under Lt Col. W.T. HENT R.F.A) became the 19th Div Arty CENTRE GROUP.	
"	Feb 3	AT 9.0 h.m.	The RIGHTGROUP took over A B & D batteries 155 Bde R.F.A from the CENTRE GROUP. The RIGHTGROUP then covered the front held by the 57th Inf Bde. The front was divided up into zones as follows.	CA

BATTERY POSITION ZONE OP

B/155 M20d 68 46 K23d46 – K23b6500 K2.d0777
A/155 M37a 14 K23b6500 – K23d7530 K27a18
D/166 K26a16 K23d7530 – K29d46 K27d3075
B/166 K26b04 K29d46 – K29d16 K2.a744
C/168 K27c27 K29d16 – K29a0 K27a50
D/155 K26a29 K23a46 – K23d6500 K2b.0010
D/166 K27a0055 K23b6500 – K29dB.0 M21C90

Army Form C. 2118.

WAR DIARY
or
INTELLIGENCE SUMMARY.
(Erase heading not required.)

B117

Hour, Date, Place	Summary of Events and Information	Remarks and references to Appendices
MARTINSART. Feby 1st 1916.	Heavy artillery bombardment at 1.35 p.m. between THIEPVAL WOOD and river hand. Enemy's DMG (Trench) Mortar opened fire. PEAKE DIVISION own Battery opposite THIEPVAL Fired 20 rounds of THIEPVAL. Selo expended 245. Billets (Mess) 25 hvy. Shelles 7 TM mortars around THIEPVAL.	
MARTINSART. Feb. 2nd 1916.	Enemy artillery fire. Enemy TM Mortars. Enemy Rifle Grenades fired at THIEPVAL (south) in Revetier Sap at THIEPVAL (north) new Salient THIEPVAL CHATEAU & South Eastern of THIEPVAL - made a lot of noise. Nearly T THIEPVAL also fired a round or two of shells expended. 90	
MARTINSART. Feb. 3rd 1916.	Enemy artillery fire. Enemy's hood field of scores intermittent during the day to which our replies in same kind. Note Enemy shewn was near PONTER LE GRAND at 1 pm from 10 end of to-day. People with British (at 4.30 pm) Peuplars officially from General Division shots.	BAB

WAR DIARY
or
INTELLIGENCE SUMMARY.

(Erase heading not required.)

Army Form C. 2118.

Hour, Date, Place	Summary of Events and Information	Remarks and references to Appendices
MARTINSART. Feb 3/16 (Cont'd)	Our B/155 Battery position beaten zone 6 times to-day. German trench again beaten zone 92.	
MARTINSART. Feb 4/16.	Enemy heavily shelling THIEPVAL WOOD AUTHUILLE and THIEPVAL WOOD. Several direct hits on front line trenches. The Regiment retaliated and fired on German working parties near R/25 B 8/1. Violent shelling continued. Reports from R.F.C. we Pts. 905 [illegible] and 3549 at N.E. [illegible]	
MARTINSART. 2.A. 5/16.	Enemy artillery more active and shelled P.N. also THIEPVAL WOOD, AUTHUILLE and THIEPVAL WOOD. Our guns could do no shoot to-day. The lines on the German wire around [illegible] again to-day not equally	

WAR DIARY or INTELLIGENCE SUMMARY

(Erase heading not required.)

Army Form C. 2118

Hour, Date, Place	Summary of Events and Information	Remarks and references to Appendices
MARTINSART 24.5/16 (Contd)	Good weather. At 10.30 am & 12.10 pm. British aeroplanes shelled — one by S/S bracket — on silenced by 6th Balloon. Afternoon dull & quiet. During the day enemy's fire slackened. Hostile aeroplanes active, about 750. 4 groups of batteries.	
MARTINSART 25.5/16	Enemy battery very active. O/S shown by front line at Serre. B/Maj (How.) Bty, my other bty at P31c 50.85 — Bty at Chins Trench Q2d97. B25B — Battery at R25d c95.45 another at R29.18 by aeroplane. See day Col's Cmd by R Bs B — Fired on and disposed of. Sent Lt Col W.8. R Buchan Left the command 15 act as Adjutant Lt Gen Staff. Lieutenant Col W.8. R Buchan REAOVHA O/C 168 Bde RFA assumed command in Lt Col Bunbury's absence.	RBB

WAR DIARY
INTELLIGENCE SUMMARY
Army Form C. 2118.

Hour, Date, Place	Summary of Events and Information	Remarks and references to Appendices
MARTINSART. Feb 7/7/16	Enemy shelled trench South of MARTINSART. Enemy trenches shelled from about 2030 onwards on the North bk THIEPVAL ROAD - French 30 minutes rapid fire. Battery (How?) B/152 fired 16 rounds shrapnel into position about R.31.c.85.05. He also shelled shrapnel into the shelled L'AVOCOURT Rd - Ron Lyons trenches R.25.B.7.5. 3/152 fired fifty Cemetery Bank at R.27.B.6.3 Observed working parts at R.27. treaty good. No Rifle shells expended. 92. shells expended. 92. Enemy shelled G.2 section between 2 and 11am down dumps & trenches at various rates. The three very little during the day.	
MARTINSART. 2.b 9/16 It 9/16.	B/152 (How?) Btly fires on Hun and Supplies Post at R.31.a.35.45 and R.25.D.20.95. D/152 fires 50 rounds shrapnel at large body of troops in Regina to Staufen trenches. Groups of Regiment of Bavarian Infantry were found in during the day.	AARS

WAR DIARY
or
INTELLIGENCE SUMMARY.
(Erase heading not required.)

Army Form C. 2118.

Instructions regarding War Diaries and Intelligence Summaries are contained in F.S. Regs., Part II and the Staff Manual respectively. Title pages will be prepared in manuscript.

Hour, Date, Place	Summary of Events and Information	Remarks and references to Appendices
MARTINSART 9th Feb/16. (contd)	Enemy's artillery quiet. Our Lts [?] offers Stilly during the day. Little heavy. Wounded 9 ms C. Our shell expended 208	
MARTINSART 10 Feb/16.	At 2pm - 3pm and 4.30 pm the Batteries R.3 light T.M. Battery [?] shelled[?] [illegible] at R.3 & [?] same [?] Two different[?] [?] batteries. Enemy's T.M.'s 39 rounds. Shelled [?] [?] our [?]. Mortaring active. [?] [?] replies 8 batteries 86 & 22 in [?] and [?] [?] retaliation 62.24 [?] observation [?] during the day. Hostile another T.M. near [?] lively. Mortar had reply to Berles [?] town and caused [?] [?] observer in [?]. Report of GROUP Infantry. Fired if enemy infantry heard [?] [?] [?] Kent observed trenches [?] Shells fire during day 139.	RAB

Forms/C. 2118/10.

WAR DIARY or INTELLIGENCE SUMMARY

Army Form C. 2118.

(Erase heading not required.)

Hour, Date, Place	Summary of Events and Information	Remarks and references to Appendices
MARTINSART. 11. Feb. 16.	Enemy's artillery and trench mortars ranged on A.2, G.2 Subs. Some of the shots falling into MARTINSART, which killed and wounded one officer and four men. Our artillery and trench mortar officers replied to enemy trench mortars & effectively stopping his damage. 5th and 6th heavier guns.	
MARTINSART. 12. Feb. 16.	Between 8.30 and 9.30 PM enemy heavily shelled with trench mortars our entire A.E. from THIEPVAL WOOD — Exclusive — right up to river — BOUZINCOURT. Main aid RANK again shelled at Q.11.b. A.H.S.Y. showed fire very than ordinarily. Much of the shells as usual were blind. Our Artillery fire was not as of enemy trenches. Our Artillery fire with effect on enemy trenches damaging the banks & parapets. Shells exploded at the heather road.	[signature]

WAR DIARY or INTELLIGENCE SUMMARY

Hour, Date, Place	Summary of Events and Information	Remarks and references to Appendices
MARTINSART 13.26/6/16 (Co Z.E.)	Brigade Reconn. Coln. moved from Contay to Martinsart. Orders received for action to Brigade to move out of billets and take entrenchment, guns by platoons and Ridley to be landed, one gun by 2nd Hants, Ridley gun (Btty. Reec (Beaulieu Farm Trench) B/Hanks and B/Essex (New) Btte 16 guns in action also B/15th men in the new Trench	
MARTINSART 13.2d.d.16.	Month shelled with 4.5 and 5.9's at intervals during the day. Rifle & Tr: bn 2 Lebro shelter about 11 am at the back of Lemon - AUTHUILLE and AIRLEY WOOD shelled between 4 and 5 pm to the right of the billets. MUSS caught a hare running from the direction of FERME DU MOUQUET. Enemy trench mortars active heavier guns fired about 120.	

WAR DIARY or INTELLIGENCE SUMMARY

Army Form C. 2118.

Hour, Date, Place	Summary of Events and Information	Remarks and references to Appendices
MARTINSART. 14. Feb. 16	MESNIL, MESNIL CHATEAU & AVELUY WOOD shelled at intervals. Enemy mortars quiet, also enemy's artillery, with the exception of G.1.2.- G.1. Suits heavily shelled between 2 and 2.30. Our Batteries replied on to Hem Ringelin and did much damage to enemy's parapets in the shell dropped in MARTINSART. No fires up working parties near [illegible] in any [illegible] effect. Shells expended 25. The Batn. Hdqrs. Staff (excepting Adjutant & 2 orderlies) proceeded to [illegible] being relieved	
FRECHENCOURT. 14. 21. 16.	FRECHENCOURT at 10 a.m. on 16th inst. The Right Half Bn. on 16th inst. O/C (Lt Col Oldham) remains at MARTINSART with O/C (C.Bty) acting as Brady officer until morning of 16th inst. Half section of each Battery came out of action in the afternoon and proceeded to FRECHENCOURT. Half place of rest in MONTIGNY 16 to be effect. Head place of rest is MONTIGNY and not FRECHENCOURT-	

WAR DIARY
INTELLIGENCE SUMMARY.
(Erase heading not required.)

Army Form C. 2118.

Hour, Date, Place	Summary of Events and Information	Remarks and references to Appendices
MARTINSART. 15.Feb.'16	Enemy artillery very quiet. Several Trench Mortars fired into our Left (62 Brigade) registered trenches throughout the day. Our new Battery fired into trenches in reply to Trench Mortars and grenades & weather fair. Shells expended, 226.	
FRÉCHENCOURT and MONTIGNY	Remainder & half-section of Battery proceeded to MONTIGNY with remainder of them respective Battery Staffs. Brigade Hd. to Staff, Amb. Col. and half section of Battalion moved at 1.30 p.m. to MONTIGNY from FRÉCHENCOURT as ordered.	
MONTIGNY. 16.Feb.'16.	Zone handed over. 9 a.m. 16th inst. Lt.Col. OBham A.D.A. statues to his Brigade and the Regt. and remainder of Hd. Qr. Staff proceeded to MONTIGNY.	
MONTIGNY 17th to 20th Feb.'16	Brigade in rest- hies occupied by all H.Q. Btys. and A.S.Col. in cleaning up &c.	

WAR DIARY
or
INTELLIGENCE SUMMARY.
(Erase heading not required.)

Army Form C. 2118.

Hour, Date, Place	Summary of Events and Information	Remarks and references to Appendices
MONTIGNY. 21. Feb. '16. to 29. Feb. '16.	Lt. Col. Sr. St. P. Rumbow returned to the Brigade from BEAUVAL (School of Gunnery). From this date to 29th Feb. '16 the Brigade has occupied in redrilling, Gun laying, riding and driving drill etc. Gas instruction. On 28th. Orders received by Officer Comdg. Brigade to relieve 83rd. Brigade R.F.A. in action, on 3rd March. Preparations for the move commenced, and everything made ready.	

32nd Divisional Artillery.

155th BRIGADE R. F. A.

MARCH 1 9 1 6

Army Form C. 2118.

WAR DIARY
or
INTELLIGENCE SUMMARY.
(Erase heading not required.)

155th Brigade R.F.A.

Hour, Date, Place	Summary of Events and Information	Remarks and references to Appendices
MONTIGNY. 1 March '16.	Brigade in rest. Getting ready to proceed at ALBERT. R.O. Battery Circle sent forward to Battery position at 83°. Brigade to prepare to take over guns after to be left at horses one to R.O. R.M. and one gun limbers come to 83° Pole. R.M. & Col Earley the Brigade went to Heights (83°0) with R.Col Earley in Chargers [?] the Battery 20th Pothencourt Suttons closed. (Lt Col & Pothencourts organization Sunday.	
MONTIGNY. 2 Royal '16 to ALBERT	6 Battery Staff proceeded to ALBERT and remains of Battery came on later. Ligne came billeted as follows: ALBERT. R. Pontigny - ALBERT. B.M.C. do - MOULIN-DE-VIVIER. Headquarters Staff proceeded to farm Rolle. The Nation Officer on a bicycle) and Asst Adjt Officer, the Medical Officer also came slowly. Find quarters helped Liains in ALBERT (men to Station.)	

WAR DIARY
INTELLIGENCE SUMMARY

Army Form C. 2118.

155th Brigade RFA

Hour, Date, Place	Summary of Events and Information	Remarks and references to Appendices
ALBERT. 3rd March 16	Lt. Col. Cunliffe and Adjt. 83rd Bde RFA arrived at HQ 155 Bde at 1.30 p.m. The Batteries also took over the Brs 83rd Bde RFA guns and horses and war diaries etc. No. 1 and Left Section (the returned our mistake) Officers & No. 2 and Right Section (83rd Bde Officers Then returned to Albert with their to form alt telephone signallers & dug-outs near standard single lines to the artillery. Left the form B/166 (Howr) Bty. together B/Ventry (Howr) and C/155 also formed the C/as with B and C/155 Bde return to command by Lt. Col. Grant Suttie. Br P Bushby RFA from today D/155 still in action near RIVELLY under command of 49th Brigade.	19AB

WAR DIARY
or
INTELLIGENCE SUMMARY.

(Erase heading not required.)

Army Form C. 2118.

155 Brigade RFA.

Hour, Date, Place	Summary of Events and Information	Remarks and references to Appendices
ALBERT. 4th March 16.	Arrangements made for B/155 to come under the 6th Divn from to-day, and B/168 to join here this Group - also the 2 Section of D/155. Battery to be moved so that B/168 (my Battery No 23 D + 4) from N.39.c.45.70 - B/168 taking that Battery position B.20/155 and B/155 (now B/168) (now? B/185) in action at following points: B/155 - C/155 - B/168 - Weather very windy - sun shining from time to time only during day and night. Enemy artillery rather active on A27 and A53 feet. Enemy of our Batteries of this Group firing upon the enemy trenches in their break that occurred until good effect. 370 rounds (about) expended in this bombardment. Several roads & area were active during the day seen near to the frontal trench observation balloons observed this day. Stella rockets 390	
ALBERT. 5 March 16.	Lieut Logan admitted to Hospital suffering from wound. Epsom - Scot.	

RAB

WAR DIARY *or* **INTELLIGENCE SUMMARY.**

Army Form C. 2118.

55th Brigade R.F.A.

Hour, Date, Place	Summary of Events and Information	Remarks and references to Appendices
ALBERT. 6 March 16.	Owing to standing orders changing at short notice (army to Corps) B/Bat (How?) 745 fired on enemy Batts at Infantry request. Enemy artillery active - they put about 30 rounds of 10.5cm & a like number of x.13cm at Observer post. Observation Balloons during the day. A few shells fell in ALBERT - no damage done. PZIBERT - no damage done. Enemy aircraft still fairly active around PZIBERT - BZIETRE - POOS. Shells expended 36.	
ALBERT. 7 March 16.	Hostile fire. A + D/155 very active in every sector - also B/Bat (How?) Reg. Enemy artillery rather active - a number of shells put into PZIBERT from N.E. and intermittently into E5 D.21 (Off.) & LA BOISSELLE. Shells fired 129. Several observation Balloons of + (shown?)	

WAR DIARY

Army Form C. 2118.

INTELLIGENCE SUMMARY. 155th Brigade, R.F.A.

(Erase heading not required.)

Instructions regarding War Diaries and Intelligence Summaries are contained in F.S. Regs., Part II. and the Staff Manual respectively. Title pages will be prepared in manuscript.

Hour, Date, Place	Summary of Events and Information	Remarks and references to Appendices
8 March /16. ALBERT.	Weather fine & clear. A special shoot took place as follows:- C/155- Battery 20 Rds. H.E. fired Trenches x Sc 5302 to x Sc 6302 to damage enemy Trenches. A/155 to x B/155 Registered 21 Rds. H.E. on x 14a 3581 & damage dugouts. B/155 (How) Regd. 60 Rds. H.E. on Trench Junctions and against 119 Bois Squre - to demolish dugouts. B/155- 33 Rds. Shrapnel H.E. fired on enemy trenches & result mostly too short. D Battery Regd. 56 H/32a 9385 with effect. Supports by B/155 Bty Enemy Batterys quiet, so few small Tache were fired, and own Trenches got a few in particular east of ALBERT.	
9 March 1916. ALBERT.	The Cal. Grant two very slow rounds during the day. Enemy Battery inactive except for a burst of H.E. about 50 Rds.) on trenches & opposite OVILLERS. Trent Mortar fire rather more and met. Stella fired 13 -	

Army Form C. 2118.

155th Brigade, R.F.A.

WAR DIARY
INTELLIGENCE SUMMARY
(Erase heading not required.)

Hour, Date, Place	Summary of Events and Information	Remarks and references to Appendices
10. March 16. ALBERT.	Enemy Trench Mortars & Machine Guns & Artillery active. Rifle replies ineffective with Shrapnel & H.E. Weather dull rain later. Total Rounds fired 266.	
11. March 1916.	A large hostile Biplane reported flying over F.S.S. Section at 11.10 am. It returned very shortly afterwards upon being met by anti-aircraft guns. Our Artillery fire intermittent during day to registrate Battery on F2, F3 & F1 sectors doing very little damage. Enemy Trench Mortars very active, aeroplanes & artillery to their fire unit got Rounds on enemy trenches the day is — 3/Hoy (How) — 106; B/155 — 40; Battery 156 — 20; B/155 — H.E. — at 5 Bows in the unit — this battery sent 6 into an enemy trench to destroy sandbags and material work. Captain Barker reported posted to 5th of Brigade and assumed command of the Brigade. Lieut. R.R. Burwell relinquished his duties as Adjutant & Orderly Officer and assumed that of Adjutant. Lieut. Mr. Jones transferred from "D" Battery of the Brigade. Lieut R. Mayo appointment as Orderly Officer. Lieut R. Mayo Hospital Sick (Menongitis).	

Army Form C. 2118.

WAR DIARY
or
INTELLIGENCE SUMMARY.
(Erase heading not required.)

155th Brigade, R.F.A.

Hour, Date, Place	Summary of Events and Information	Remarks and references to Appendices
12th March ALBERT.	Enemy artillery fairly active throughout the day. ALBERT and Bray, possibly and commung Trenches to Fourk . Few new sites. Shells 4.2 up to 5" and ? (about 450-770) m.m. shells. We Silenced 5.9 Bry. (about) firing down the line upon Kevel work and damaged Gun emplacement. Fired 250 rounds, machine gun Trenches, Route & Shortly effective. D/155 Bty fired on enemy Trenches at OVILLERS with good effect.	
13th March ALBERT.	Several hostile observation balloons up during the day. Intermittent shelling & various tasks up the line during the day. Enemy Batteries in the BOISSELET very active to which we replied with 18 pr Shrapnel, also D/155 fired 200 Rds Shrapnel on more enemy with good trenches X.7.B (OVILLERS) also B/155 - 220 Rds Shrapnel wire cutting at X13a Cat 1.A. BOISSELET. 31/16e (How) Bty fired 62 Rds H.E. to damage dugouts & enemy Trench at X.7.B OVILLERS. Weather - good.	

WAR DIARY
INTELLIGENCE SUMMARY

Army Form C. 2118.

1st Brigade R.F.A.

(Erase heading not required.)

Hour, Date, Place	Summary of Events and Information	Remarks and references to Appendices
14 March 16. ALBERT	Enemy artillery fairly active. Our howitzers put 1/10 on OWLERS wood shelled at 2 pm with 30 pdr. & 4 pdr. shell. Trench mortars & machine guns active during the day and night. 16" shots (Bosh) applied at 14 Bde Stafford + R.A. Billets (Hown) MPAH Pres 70 Rds H.E. on HENU, also on FM at + 13d 8 · 3 · 2 · 7 pm. Bosch open fire well during afternoon to East of POZIERES. Enemy aeroplane was seen flying in direction of STILLERS to ALBERT at 9 pm. Weather clear & fair.	
15 March. ALBERT	He entered our BOIZELLE Front trenches with 18pdr H.E. around 4th BOIZELLE Trench Junction directed at + 14c. (4A BOIZELLE) Enemy Artillery quiet, only showing any activity on stations. Capt Gunn R.A.M.C. Canadian R. Battery got slight concussion — R. Battery got Private wounded — admitted to hospital.	

R.A.A

WAR DIARY / INTELLIGENCE SUMMARY

155th Brigade R.F.A.

Army Form C. 2118.

Hour, Date, Place	Summary of Events and Information	Remarks and references to Appendices
16th March. ALBERT.	Communication trenches from ALBERT to BOUZINCOURT Road shelled with somewhat little effect during the day - also E2 & E3. Enemy trenches (our batteries replying to hostile batteries) in many trenches A/155 and B/155 on Railway Dump at X & B (in OVILLERS). Enemy Railway Junction at Zenker Graben shelled by D/155 & Divisional Group. Heavy enemy Trench Mortars active from POZIERES, CONTALMAISON & THIEPVAL & Hand Grenade Battery.	
17th March. ALBERT.	A few long shells fired into ALBERT and lost our artillery made a reply. We replied and carried Heavier gun Rounds fired 150.	
18th March. ALBERT.	A quiet day. Everything fire a few rounds at intervals with little effect. Byelan (New) DG again fires to Ry Rd in the damage French Batave in L19 BOISSELLE. Enemy Trench Mortars became active at the 30 night but soon finding we had put H.E. into the Trenches Placed into H.E. into Trenches	R.W.C.

Army Form C. 2118.

WAR DIARY
INTELLIGENCE SUMMARY
(Erase heading not required.)

155th Brigade - R.F.A.

Hour, Date, Place	Summary of Events and Information	Remarks and references to Appendices
19th Sept. POZIERES.	19/11/15 - Fire on trenches in LA BOISELLE - wire cutting - 225 rounds Shell. Refugees in quiet. Trench Mortars stopped activity to which our Trench Mortars and Artillery replied, and silenced them. Bty J.J. 20 Rds H.E. on enemy observation Post. Trenches established in trench strong in front of Trenches. New sites prepared. Rate of fire day & night: 20 gns. rounds expended 279.	
20th Sept. POZIERES.	Enemy artillery rather active - several rounds heavy shells were fired into POZIERES. Many more 15 cm. shells on our being fired into the vicinity of POZIERES and CONTALMAISON. 9" - directed fire on new 15 cm Battery in hour bright up to this afternoon. Enemy fire in front of the caused fire in front of LA BOISSELLE at 5.30 from Lewis Trench Mortar sent down to which we replied with T.Ms. & 18 Pdr. Shells. Transport good. Shells expended 324.	

(73989) W4141-463. 400,000. 9/14. H.&J., Ltd. Forms/C. 2118/10.

Army Form C. 2118.

155th Brigade R.F.A.

WAR DIARY
or
INTELLIGENCE SUMMARY
(Erase heading not required.)

Instructions regarding War Diaries and Intelligence Summaries are contained in F.S. Regs., Part II and the Staff Manual respectively. Title pages will be prepared in manuscript.

Hour, Date, Place	Summary of Events and Information	Remarks and references to Appendices
21. March. ALBERT.	5.0 - 7.7 pm. Shells fired into our trenches opposite LA BOISSELLE at 2mm. otherwise quiet all day. Light organised shoots of the Retaive the signal nightly to silence Enemy trenches firing. Shells fired. 265.	
22. March. ALBERT.	Enemy artillery much more active. Farms entire shells very heavy into our trenches 152.E.3.7. (F. Sector) from 2.25 till 4.30. At 4.15 pm with 126 RdS a sharp bre Shrapnel & H.E. attack, a clear wire was made there. After which Battns. were active again, firing on OVILLERS replacement located from a lorry in Baulie. The house was shelled & demolished opened fire 516.	

Army Form C. 2118.

WAR DIARY
or
INTELLIGENCE SUMMARY.
(Erase heading not required.)

15th Brigade A.S.R.

Instructions regarding War Diaries and Intelligence Summaries are contained in F.S. Regs., Part II and the Staff Manual respectively. Title pages will be prepared in manuscript.

Hour, Date, Place	Summary of Events and Information	Remarks and references to Appendices
23rd March. ALBERT.	Enemy artillery quiet — a few shells (97M/m) only. Enemy fired into our billets during day. B/155 Battery was again engaged at Hostile Battery on enemy trenches at 1/25. Rounds were exchanged at intervals but was silenced with our fire. Two machine guns supposed to be located in OVILLERS (Mon Lavern) were seen & destroyed as far as could be observed. No enemy working parts were observed in OVILLERS & when dispersed with our fire. Shells expended 300.	
24th March. ALBERT.	A very quiet day — very few shells exchanged. Billets supplied one scout at 19 BOISELLE in preparation for scheme on 26th inst. Shells expended 31. 1 Hostile Party Cpl. Banks. Lieut. Hurst admitted to Hospital.	
25th March. ALBERT.	B/155 Bty reported firing 80 Rds. Shrapnel + HE. on wire on enemy's wire. B/155 185. 100 Rds - All in Trench — but not heavy. Every rifleman on ALBERT. Shells expended 206. Weather fair.	RBB

(73989) W4141—463. 400,000. 9/14. H.&J.Ltd. Forms/C. 2118/10.

WAR DIARY

INTELLIGENCE SUMMARY

(Erase heading not required.)

Army Form C. 2118.

155th Brigade, R.F.A.

Hour, Date, Place	Summary of Events and Information	Remarks and references to Appendices
26th March. ALBERT.	Show rounds were fired by the Batteries from the Canister fire. Hun Guns at 4 pm. Enemy fired 12 shells into ALBERT. About 200 into our trenches. He did not reply heavily on the front rows were out to commence at 12.15 am. 27th inst. Several Very lights observed over enemy lines at night.	
27th March. ALBERT.	At 12.27 am our Batteries started bombardment of Hun trenches at LA BOISSELLE as follows:— A/155 Battery fired 129 Rds on X8c/1250 6 X 8a 0555. B " " 186 " +13 d. C " " 188 " +13 d. 15 +x14c D " " 170 " +13 d. " 53 " +13 d at 14 c B/164 (How) Bty. Hr. raid carried out in 27 Sqr. otherwise quiet. D/164 also left extra 27 Sqr Batteries — O/Leap, while the bombardment was on the by/Rly raided the Hun trenches — gaining access to the Huns cut fire, the Huns trenches made by the Batteries knocking down enemy reptile Very many dug outs Sections and the Rallye were also by Hun trench-fire. Shells expended 700 trench-fire.	

WAR DIARY

INTELLIGENCE SUMMARY.

(Erase heading not required.)

Army Form C. 2118.

155. Brigade R.F.A.

Hour, Date, Place	Summary of Events and Information	Remarks and references to Appendices
28th March. ALBERT.	Enemy Artillery and Trench Mortars active in F.2 and 1.3 Sectors. Our guns fired very little during the day on account of infantry relief. Enemy did not attempt any move in front of trenches in front of F.2 Sector. Shells expended 12. Weather good.	
29. March ALBERT.	Enemy Artillery quiet – also Trench Mortars. Several enemy aeroplanes were active during the day – neither were forced down. Our R.F.A. guns dispersed several working parties. D/155 (How.) Bty fires 18 Bty: Ven enemy trenches also to destroy Barrage. Shells expended 158. Weather good –	
30. March. ALBERT.	Enemy artillery & trench mortars fairly active on our trenches. He replies during the day with shrapnel & H.E. – working parties dispersed by our fire. Hostile Harass over ALBERT quiet – driven back with A.A. guns. Shells expended 79. Weather good –	

Army Form C. 2118.

1st Res. R.F.A.

WAR DIARY
INTELLIGENCE SUMMARY
(Erase heading not required.)

Hour, Date, Place	Summary of Events and Information	Remarks and references to Appendices
31. March ALBERT	Enemy artillery quiet. Our guns fire on several nearby points. Visibility poor from Hostle flares. Enemy driven from our Pt. 87.25 with R.H. guns. D/155 Bty. dislodges a map in Pine - signalling - by Verey Lights at him. Blue bombs seen at Fricourt pats of the enemy trenches break good - hostile reported 45.	

P. A. Dansell
Lt. M. F. for Lt. Colonel R.F.A.
Comdg. 155th R. F. Brigade, R.F.A.

Army Form C. 2118.

WAR DIARY
INTELLIGENCE SUMMARY.
(Erase heading not required.)

155. Brigade R.F.A.

Hour, Date, Place	Summary of Events and Information	Remarks and references to Appendices
ALBERT 1 April 1/16.	Enemy artillery quiet. Enemy trench mortars active during the early hours of the morning. C/155 retaliated to them with 26A and 15AK. Our guns inflicted several casualties on enemy transport. Hostile plane came over in the direction of Bécourt but returned under fire from our A.A. guns. Shells expended 107 - Weather good. Orders received that the 32nd Div are to be relieved by the 8th Div (III Corps) 155th Bde RFA to move to Bs RUBEMPRE on the 7th April.	
ALBERT 2 April 1916	Enemy artillery fairly active on ALBERT. Our artillery very active in retaliation to enemy Trench Mortars and unusually quiet today. No new work taken in hand today. Hostile toried ton its ascendare over ALBERT driven back by our A.A. guns. Weather clear in my light. Shells expended 128.	
ALBERT 3 April 1916	Enemy artillery very quiet. Our artillery active in retaliation to hostile Trench mortars and in support of 7 pairs of the 8th (relieving) division. Hostile observation balloon up during the morning. Weather clear. Shells expended 129.	EJC

Army Form C. 2118.

WAR DIARY
or
INTELLIGENCE SUMMARY.
(Erase heading not required.)

155th Brigade RFA

Hour, Date, Place	Summary of Events and Information	Remarks and references to Appendices
ALBERT April 4th 1916	Hostile artillery not very active. Our artillery fired on enemy machine gun emplacements and in retaliation to hostile trench mortars. B/155 (How) fired 228x in new emplacements. Enemy Aeroplane balloon up early (?) afternoon. Neuport activity. Ammunition expended 175 rounds.	
ALBERT April 5th 1916	Very little activity by the enemy artillery. Our artillery only active in reply to hostile trench mortars. Weather very misty making observation difficult. Bombs fired 85.	
ALBERT April 6th 1916	Enemy artillery quiet. Our artillery active in retaliation to trench mortar activity. (?) Enemy very busy working (?) together. Rounds expended - 148. Gun positions of all the batteries in the Brigade were advanced 70yds in a rearward direction (re-sited ?) by : 1st Battery A/155 assisted by 1st Battery B/155 " 3rd Battery C/155 " O Battery R.H.A. D/155 " 5th Battery Battery of 155 "Bde" left their new position & took over the (?) of existing Batteries. Relief (?) of Batteries proceeded to new map reference. The independent (155 Bde) take over by the 5th (?) part of the (?) part of the 3rd Div. Group commanded Lt Col Butler R.H.A. whose headquarters is there (?) at Albert today.	G.T. 6/4

Army Form C. 2118.

WAR DIARY
or
INTELLIGENCE SUMMARY.
(Erase heading not required.)

153rd Bde RFA

Hour, Date, Place	Summary of Events and Information	Remarks and references to Appendices
ALBERT April 7th 1916	Enemy shelled our front line trenches with 77 m.m. (about 34 rds) between 9.0 am & 12.0 noon. We expended 20 rounds in retaliation & system of relieving tourers. The Brigade HQ Staff with the exception of Telephonists moved to RUBEMPRÉ under the Orderly Officer, at 10.0 AM. Sections released by the 5th Bde RHA. Remaining sections of batteries marched to RUBEMPRÉ on being relieved at 7.0 PM. Lt Col Holt P Bembery proceeded to ST NLIS to take over the duties of C.R.A. 32nd Div. on arrival. The above'd Brig Gen. T.R. Lyle. Capt. R.B. Newton C/153 proceeded to ST NLIS to take over duties of Brigade Major 32nd Div. R.A. during the absence thereof of Capt Algeo. The 2nd Lieut of the Cmds gp of 32 Div. RA (153rd Bde) have handed over at 7.0 PM to Lys group commanded 5th Divl RA. Weather very good.	[signature]
RUBEMPRÉ (Beauval Cya) 8th April 1916 to 12th April 1916 (inclusive)	During this period Brigade engaged in cleaning up & drill parade &c. On account of watering place being 4 miles from RUBEMPRÉ 1 instructions were received for Brigade to move to CONTAY on 13th April 1916.	

Army Form C. 2118.

155 Brigade R.F.A.

WAR DIARY
or
INTELLIGENCE SUMMARY.
(Erase heading not required.)

Hour, Date, Place	Summary of Events and Information	Remarks and references to Appendices
RUBEMPRE 13 April 1916. CONTAY.	The Brigade moved to RUBEL + Colr. moving at various intervals and occupied lines & billets by 12.30 p.m.	H.Q. Staff CONTAY — 4 Batteries billeted by 12.30
CONTAY. 14 April 1916 to 27 April 1916.	Brigade in Reserve Area — time occupied cleaning-up, drill orders and general training. Advice received on 20th that Major P. Sheppard D.S.O. is appointed Lt.Col. to 1st Pierre Bruton R.F.A. to take command of the Brigade. Major P. Sheppard D.S.O. R.F.A. arrived on 26.4.16.	
CONTAY. 28.4.16.	The Brigade paraded at 2.p.m in Relief Service Marching Order, & was inspected by the new Officer Comdg. & — recorded took 115 N.C.O.s + men were away in digging parties. Major P. Sheppard D.S.O. R.F.A. took over command of the Brigade on this date.	RAR

Army Form C. 2118.

WAR DIARY
of
INTELLIGENCE SUMMARY.
(Erase heading not required.)

1st Brigade RFA

Instructions regarding War Diaries and Intelligence Summaries are contained in F.S. Regs., Part II. and the Staff Manual respectively. Title pages will be prepared in manuscript.

Hour, Date, Place	Summary of Events and Information	Remarks and references to Appendices
CONTAY. 29.4.16.	Brigade engaged in cleaning up - drill parades & general training.	
CONTAY. 30.4.16.	Lt. Col. R.F. Rivers Bulkeley DSO. landed at command of this Bde. in not. Major P. Sheppard DSO. F.R.F.A. Bde. left for Review at 5.30am. en route for England.	

J. Shepherd
Major RFA
Comdg 1st Bde RFA.

RGAB

32nd Divisional Artillery.

155th BRIGADE R. F. A.

M A Y 1 9 1 6

WAR DIARY
INTELLIGENCE SUMMARY
(Erase heading not required.)

Army Form C. 2118.

155th Brigade R.F.A.

BRB

Hour, Date, Place	Summary of Events and Information	Remarks and references to Appendices
CONTAY 1.5.16.	The Brigade is in the Reserve Area. Seven Officers and Drivers + two Officers attached to other Brigades of the 32nd Division for gun drill. O.B. is digging. The remainder of the Brigade engaged in cleaning up of the 32nd training —drill re. NCOs + men of Divisional Ammn Coln attend to the 152 whilst Brigade in Reserve Area for instruction in gun drill. Regtl Sgt Major handed to England on 18.4/16. Regt Sgt Major A.J. Baker No. 12366, Joined the Brigade on 18-5-16. Btt. Sgt Major T. Davis transferred from B. Battery to England on 20/4/16. The following postings + transfers took place during the month:— 2 Lieut G. Dundas transferred from B. Battery to Y 32 Trench Mortar Battery from 7/5/15.	

WAR DIARY
INTELLIGENCE SUMMARY

Army Form C. 2118.

155th Brigade R.F.A.

Hour, Date, Place	Summary of Events and Information	Remarks and references to Appendices
COUY. 1.5.16.	Postings & Transfers (continued):— Lieut Hunt to "B" Battery from 4.3" Trench Mortar Battery from 9/5/16. Lieut C.L. Paul taken on strength of Brigade and attached to "A" Battery — 29.4.16. Lieut F. Holliday transferred from "D" Battery to "B" Battery & to be in command — 26.4.16. Sergt E. de Mairshe joins the Brigade 20/5/16 and appointed a Battery Sgt Major B. Battery. Sgt. T. Dunsby joined the Brigade 20/5/16 and appointed a Battery Sgt Major A Battery. Sergt H.S. Tate joined the Brigade 9/5/16 and appointed a Bty Sgt Major to C. Battery 9/5/16 On 14th/5/16. a working party from A B and C. Batteries was sent to before [...] an Officer dug-outs in at Q. 35 b. and 2 — an Officer in charge of each Battery working party, materials obtained from R.E. Dump at AVELUY.	9199

WAR DIARY

INTELLIGENCE SUMMARY

55th Brigade RFA

Army Form C. 2118.

Hour, Date, Place	Summary of Events and Information	Remarks and references to Appendices
CONTAY	Lieut E. Roberts transferred from Amn Colm to 161 Brigade RFA on 13/5/16. Trench Bridges having been made to = scale of 2 to per Battery, the Batteries commenced practice with them over ditches. Carrying Kem', which was very satisfactory. The C-in-C General Sir Douglas Haig passed through Contay and expressed his satisfaction with the practice at "B" Battery which was favoured has [?] day -11th. 13 from 26th the Brigade Amn. Col. is broken up in accordance with re-organisation of Divisional Artillery. The personnel going (i) to 1st Cdn Col: (ii) to Heavy Trench Mortar Batteries. (iii) to medium trench Mortar Batteries. The horses are transferred to (i) to new section of DAC (ii) generally to units of 32nd and 49th Divisions and (iii) Horse	BRR

WAR DIARY
INTELLIGENCE SUMMARY
(Erase heading not required.)

Army Form C. 2118.

Hour, Date, Place	Summary of Events and Information	Remarks and references to Appendices
CONTAY. 26.5.16.	to evacuated Personal arrangements attached to 'B' Batteries of the Brigade. D/155 (B.Reln.) Battery is transferred to 'C' into the Brigade of 16th Bugade RFA as from 26.5. with A/164 (4.5 How.) Battery (15th) Brigade RFA transferred to this (15th) Brigade as from that date and is now known as D/155 (Late M/64) Battery - In this after the Battery shed its numbers distinctive to D/155 Battery. Lieut D. Miller, RFA, Comdg. the Bde. Ammn. Coln. is transf[d]. off the strength of the Brigade from 26/5/16. Lieut F D Smith AVC. is transfd. to 32? DAC as from 26/5/16 - from the Brigade Lieut. G. J. Bottomley is transfd. to "C" Battery from Bde. Ak. Coln. as from 15/5/16.	

WAR DIARY
INTELLIGENCE SUMMARY

155th Brigade R.F.A.

Place	Date	Hour	Summary of Events and Information	Remarks and references to Appendices
CONTAY	26/8/16		also turned G.I. Ammunition to A. Battery from B.A.C. on 24/8/16. Proposed authority for increase of one sub-altern to all 4-Gun Batteries (vice 18 pdr. & 4.5 How.) given under 3rd Div. Cav. letter SG-313 d/- 18/8/16. The Reserve positions selected for Batteries of the Brigade whilst in Reserve Area in the event of being required in case of enemy attack are as follows:— (i) If enemy captures the ridge from Auchonvillers—HAMEL— Battery positions Q.32.c.— O.Ps. at Q.21.D and R.27.B (ii) If enemy captures the ridge from AUCHONVILLERS to MESNIL:— Bty. positions in J.B and D — O.Ps. at N.2.D. (iii) If enemy captures trenches from AUTHUILLE—AUTHUILLE WOOD Area— Bty. positions at N.8.D and 1 Bty. at N of S.W. of Martin South Wood. O.Ps. at N.15.A. (iv) If enemy occupy valley running from THIEPVAL WOOD to South of AUTHUILLE WOOD— Battery positions in T.19.— O.Ps. N.15.A.	A/G/B

WAR DIARY
or
INTELLIGENCE SUMMARY.

155th Brigade RFA

(Erase heading not required.)

Place	Date	Hour	Summary of Events and Information	Remarks and references to Appendices
Corr 7A9	31/9/16	—	Enemy to remain in Reserve Area to Rathope have been given orders, so as to be quite prepared in case of emergency. On completion of the gun positions at M 35 B & D have any of that the Brigade will probably move into action one of the Brigades now there.	ABB

Shepherd
Lt.-Colonel. R.F.A.
Comdg. 155th W. Y. Brigade., R.F.A.

/32nd Divisional Artillery.

155th BRIGADE.

ROYAL FIELD ARTILLERY.

JUNE 1916::

INTELLIGENCE SUMMARY.

No. 5D

(Erase heading not required.)

Instructions regarding War Diaries and Intelligence Summaries are contained in F. S. Regs. Part II. and the Staff Manual respectively. Title pages will be prepared in manuscript.

Place	Date	Hour	Summary of Events and Information	Remarks and references to Appendices
CONTAY	8.6.16		Batteries started dumping ammunition after dark at new Bty positions	H
CONTAY	10.6.16		A/155 moved into position at Q.35.d.4.7 (N.E. corner of AVELUY WOOD) Trench Map/FRANCE H Sheet 57 D.S.E.	
CONTAY	11.6.16		B/155 moved into position at Q.35.d.4.8 N.E. corner of AVELUY WOOD H	
BOUZINCOURT	13.6.16		Headquarters 155 R.F.A. moved from CONTAY to BOUZINCOURT. H	
BOUZINCOURT	14.6.16		C/155 moved into position at Q.35.b.5.1. N.E. corner of AVELUY WOOD H	
BOUZINCOURT	19.6.16		Dumping of ammunition completed. A, B, & C dumps contained 5000 rounds. D battery dump contains 3700 rounds.	Eff.

INTELLIGENCE SUMMARY.

No. 51

(Erase heading not required.)

Place	Date	Hour	Summary of Events and Information	Remarks and references to Appendices
BOUZINCOURT	20.6.16	4.9pm	A/155 & B/155 registered on German Support line and came into trenches South of THIEPVAL. 9.2" & 8" How. covered the fire of these batteries by shelling THIEPVAL & over.	E.H.
BOUZINCOURT	22.6.16		The Brigade wagon lines concentrated just West of SENLIS	E.H.
BOUZINCOURT	23.6.16		A, B, C & D batteries came under the control of the Left Group, 32nd Divn. Artillery. (Headquarters 166 Bde. R.F.A. Lieut Col. F.T.O'Callaghan R.F.A.) Headquarters 155 Bde. R.F.A. were attached to Left Group 32nd Divn. Artly. Lieut A.R.Bonnwell (Ady 155 Bde) with 4 O.Rs. moved the Telephone exchange at Q.35 a.27. N.E. corner of AVELUY WOOD. R.S.M. J.Baker (155 Bde.R.F.A.) with 4 O.Rs. moved to Visual Signalling Post at W.10 a.55. S.W. of AVELUY WOOD.	E.H.

INTELLIGENCE SUMMARY.

No 52

(Erase heading not required.)

Place	Date	Hour	Summary of Events and Information	Remarks and references to Appendices
BOUZINCOURT	24.6.16		First day of preliminary bombardment. A, B & C Batteries cut wire on German Support line trenches S. of THIEPVAL, in second line trench South of LIGNE DES POMMES, in open of HINDENBURG REDOUBT also on a target known to hold German troops. D Battery shelled certain strong points all day	E.H.
BOUZINCOURT	25.6.16		Programme for batteries as for 24.6.16	E.H.
BOUZINCOURT	26.6.16		Left Group Headquarters (32nd Div. Arty.) moved to the "BLUFF" day out H.Q. of AUTHUILLE Q.36.c.7.8. Lt.Col. P. Sheppard D.S.O. (commands 155 Bde RFA) with 2nd Lieut F. Tootlemen (Orderly officer 155 Bde RFA) & 3 O.Rs moved to the BLUFF with Left Group Headquarters. Programme for Batteries as for 24.6.15	E.H.

INTELLIGENCE SUMMARY.

No. 53

(Erase heading not required.)

Place	Date	Hour	Summary of Events and Information	Remarks and references to Appendices
BLUFF	27/6/16		Batteries employed on wire cutting & keeping German wire already cut.	G.H.
AUTHUILLE	28/6/16		do	
BLUFF	29/6/16		Day appointed for the attack on German line. Attack postponed for 48 hours. The batteries employed on keeping wire open & shelling communication trenches & strong points.	G.H.
AUTHUILLE				
AUTHUILLE	30.6.16		Batteries employed as on 29th inst. The positions of the Batteries at the end of the month are:—	
			D/155 (How Battery) at W9d 8.5 — 150 yds S9 MARTINSART aerodrome 40° & 120°	True Bearings
			A/155 (15pr Battery) at Q35d 4.7 — N.E. corner of AVELUY WOOD — 52° & 105°	
			B/155 do at Q35d 4.6 do 43° & 77°	
			C/155 do at Q35b 5.1 do 55° & 85°	
			A, B & C Batteries are within 1500 yards of the German Front Line	

INTELLIGENCE SUMMARY.

No. 54

(Erase heading not required.)

Place	Date	Hour	Summary of Events and Information	Remarks and references to Appendices
AUTHUILLE	30.6.16 continued		which can be seen from the gun pits. A/155 has been able to cut wire on the German Front Line, laying the gun with open sights. Battery O.P.s are situated at :- A Battery W Q.35.a.26.9.5 B do Q.29.a. 3.3 C do Q.35.a. 27.9.5 D do Q.29.a. 3.3 Although A B & C batteries were in an exposed position and ammunition was brought up to them every evening during the preliminary bombardment, the battery positions & approaches to them were under intermittent heavy machine gun & artillery fire, the casualties sustained were very small. Casualties sustained from commencement of operation A/155 B/155 Nil. C/155 All map squares for want of time refer to French Map FRANCE sheet 57 D SE $\frac{1}{20,000}$ F. Shuttleworth Lt.-Colonel, R.F.A. Comdg. 155th W. L. Brigade, R.F.A.	S/A

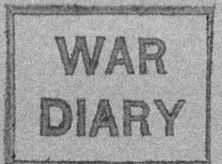

Headquarters,

155th BRIGADE, R.F.A.

(32nd Division)

J U L Y

1 9 1 6

INTELLIGENCE SUMMARY.

(Erase heading not required.) Map Reference LENS Sheet 57TRD

Title pages **55**

Place	Date	Hour	Summary of Events and Information	Remarks and references to Appendices
AUTHUILLE	1st July 1916		All batteries took part in a heavy bombardment of the enemy lines prior to the attack by the 96th infantry brigade on THIEPVAL and trenches S. of THIEPVAL. Bombardment started 65 minutes before zero hour. ZERO time was 7.30 a.m. Infantry attacked at 7.30 a.m. supported by barrages on enemy support & reserve lines. Infantry entered enemy lines & every effort made to support them but were unable to hold any enemy trenches except part of the redan.	EA
AUTHUILLE	2nd July 1916		Batteries all day engaged in shelling enemy trenches & strong points S. of THIEPVAL	EA
AUTHUILLE	3rd July 1916		All batteries bombarded heavily enemy strong points & communication trenches from 1.15 a.m to 3.0 a.m, from 5.0 a.m to 6.15 a.m. At 6.15 a.m our infantry (25th Division) attacked the enemy lines S. of THIEPVAL. The infantry attack was covered by barrages from	

INTELLIGENCE SUMMARY.

(Erase heading not required.) MAP Reference LENS Sheet 1/10,000

No 56

Place	Date	Hour	Summary of Events and Information	Remarks and references to Appendices
AUTHUILLE	July 3rd (continued)		our artillery on Enemy support & reserve lines & communication trenches. The Infantry entered enemy front line but were unable to hold it. Heavy bombardment of BUTHUILLE by the enemy after dark.	EJH
AUTHUILLE	July 4th		Little activity. Batteries fired on any enemy parties or every movement of O.P.s prevented not by anything seen. Telephone exchange & O.P.s prevented not by anything seen.	EJH
AUTHUILLE	July 5		The Enemy heavily bombarded AVELUY WOOD with H.E. & Gas Shells. Several direct hits were registered on our O.P. and at the Telephone exchange in AVELUY WOOD. LIEUT A.R.BURWELL (attd 155 Bde R.F.A) evacuated to England suffering from shell shock. 2nd/LIEUT E.FORD-JONES took over duties of Adjutant 155 Bde R.F.A.	EJH

INTELLIGENCE SUMMARY.

(Erase heading not required.) Map Reference LENS Sheet 1/40000

No 87

Place	Date	Hour	Summary of Events and Information	Remarks and references to Appendices
AUTHUILLE	July 6"		Batteries fired on Enemy communication trenches & strong points & any enemy movement seen by day. D/165 fired by night on enemy strong points	ZA
AUTHUILLE	July 7"		All batteries engaged enemy front line in front of THIEPVAL in cooperation with an attack on OVILLERS LA BOISELLE. from 7:30 a.m to 8.50 a.m. Very little enemy artillery fire could be heard. After dusk the enemy heavily shelled AUTHUILLE and E edge of AVELUY WOOD intermittently	ZA
WARLOY	July 8"		Batteries fired on any enemy movement seen. Headquarters 15 S Bde. R.F.A. moved to WARLOY. (Lt.Col. P.SHEPPARD D.S.O. and B.O.Ro.) Headquarters Wagon lines under R.S.M. BAKER remained	

INTELLIGENCE SUMMARY.

No 58 Map Reference LENS Sheet 1/10,000

Place	Date	Hour	Summary of Events and Information	Remarks and references to Appendices
WARLOY	July 8	(contd)	at SENLIS	EA
WARLOY	July 9th		Left Group 32nd Div. Batty. taken over by Lt.Col. ALLCARD D.S.O. (commanding 164 Bde R.F.A.) Left Group Headquarters moved to W.10.a.5.5. S.W. corner of AVELUY WOOD. 2/Lieut E. Ford-Jones (Adj. 155 Bde R.F.A.) posted to 155 Bde. Headquarters at WARLOY.	EA
WARLOY	July 10 1916		2/Lieut R. F. ANGAS (A/155 Bde R.F.A.) moved to WARLOY to take over duties of Orderly Officer 155.Bde. R.F.A.	EA

INTELLIGENCE SUMMARY.

No 59

(Erase heading not required.)

Place	Date	Hour	Summary of Events and Information	Remarks and references to Appendices
WARLOY	11.7.16		Batteries of the 155th Brigade R.F.A. to relieve batteries of 153rd Bde R.F.A. by section after dusk on the nights 11/12 + 12/13. A.B. & C. Batteries take over guns of A.B. & C. Batteries 153 Bde. Guns of A.B. & C. 155 to be taken to 153 Bde. wagon lines. D/153 take its own guns to the new position.	E.H.
WARLOY	12.7.16		The relief of 1 section of batteries of the 153rd Bde. was completed during the night of 11/12th without mishap.	E.H.
WARLOY	13.7.16		The relief of the second section of batteries of the 153rd Bde. by batteries of the 155th Bde. was completed during the night of the 12/13. The reliefs were completed without casualty. All ammunition dumped at the 153 Battery positions was taken over by the 155 Bde. Batteries. Batteries of 155° Bde. removed the ammunition from their	

INTELLIGENCE SUMMARY.

(Erase heading not required.) Map Reference LENS sheet 1/10,000

No. 60

Place	Date	Hour	Summary of Events and Information	Remarks and references to Appendices
WARLOY	13.7.16 (contd)		All positions to Run new positions.	
			Battery — New Position — O P	
			A/155 — Q.27.d.6.1.80 — Q.28.c.1.5	
			B/155 — Q.34.6.26.84 — Q.28.d.8.6.0	
			C/155 — Q.34.6.12.50 — Q.36.a.55.65	
			D/155 — W.4.c.34.89 — MESNIL CHATEAU	
			Batteries of 155th Bde R.F.A. were under the Right Group of 9th Division	E.T.S.
			(Lt. Col. Clifford V.D. RFA)	
WARLOY	13' to 17 July		All batteries were under the Rt. Group of the 9th Div. Artillery	S/
WARLOY	18th July		A, B, C, ||| batteries were relieved by batteries of the 9th Division. A battery moved its guns B battery left its guns in the position & took over guns (then only) from the battery who relieved it. ( ) C Battery left its guns in the position & took over guns from the relieving battery. D/155 came out of action taking its guns away. All batteries remained	

INTELLIGENCE SUMMARY.

(Erase heading not required.) Map Ref. LENS Sheet 1/100000

No. 61

Place	Date	Hour	Summary of Events and Information	Remarks and references to Appendices
WARLOY	18 July continued		at their wagon lines at SENLIS for the night	EJH
MILLY	19 July 1916		The 155th Bde. marched from SENLIS to MILLY via HEDAUVILLE - VARENNES - LEALVILLERS - LOUVENCOURT - SARTON - DOULLENS. Batteries marched at ¼ hour intervals. Brigade Headquarters & A/155 passed the starting point (Road junction ¼ mile N.E. of ☆ in SENLIS) at 6.0 a.m.; B/155 at 6.15 a.m.; C/155 at 6.30 a.m.; D/155 at 6.45 a.m. The move of the brigade was complete by 2.0 p.m. The whole of the 32 "Div. Artillery" moved, 155 Bde forming part of the Div. Arty Column. A Billeting party went on in front of the party of 1 Officer & 15 O.R's were kept behind to clear bivouacs & turn all refuse in. The weather was fine.	EJH

INTELLIGENCE SUMMARY.

(Erase heading not required.)

No. 62.   Reference LENS Sheet 1/100,000

Place	Date	Hour	Summary of Events and Information	Remarks and references to Appendices
MONCHEL	20th July 1916		The 155th Bde. marched from MILLY to MONCHEL via DOULLENS, FROHEN-LE-GRAND - VILLERS - L'HOPITAL - BOFFLES - ROUGEFAY - The Brigade was clear of MILLY by 10.0 a.m. and was in bivouac at MONCHEL by 5.0 p.m. The remainder of the 52nd Divl. Artly. bivouacd in neighbouring villages. Excellent quarters in MONCHEL. Weather fine. The Brigade marched in the following order HQ+ D/155 - C/155 - B/155. A/155	S.73
WAVRANS	21st July 1916		The 155th Bde. marched from MILLY to WAVRANS via FLERS - HARLINCOURT - RAMECOURT - ST.POL - WAVRANS. Bde. Headquarters with B/155 led followed by A/155 D/155 C/155 at½ hour intervals. The last battery was clear of MONCHEL by 8.0 am and arrived at WAVRANS at 12.0 NOON. Good working good billeting. Weather fine.	S.A

INTELLIGENCE SUMMARY

(Erase heading not required.) Of LENS shed /10000, HAZEBROUCK sheet /80000

No 63

Place	Date	Hour	Summary of Events and Information	Remarks and references to Appendices
AMES	July	22"	The Brigade marched to AMES from WAVRANS via HESTRUS-TANGRY-PRESSY-lu-PERNES-FLORINGHAM-FERFAY. Bde Hqrs with C/155 led followed at 1/4 hour intervals by D/155, B/155, B/155, The leading Battery passed the starting point (Cross roads 400 yds E.g. E.g. 2" S in HESTRUS) at 9.30 a.m. The whole Brigade were in their lines at AMES by 2.30 p.m. There is a plentiful supply of water, a stream running through the village and it is not very clean. B/155, D/155 lines are in the village, C/155 + B/155 in a large field just outside the village between AMES + BELLERY. cHz personnel are billeted in AMES. The brigade will probably remain in AMES for some days to refit + overhaul all equipment. The 32nd Divi Rty Hqrs are at ERQUEDESQUES, 161 Bde at LIERES, 164 Bde at AMETTES, 168 Bde at LESPRESSES, The 32nd DA.C. at NEDON. The Division come under I Corps Fourth Army.	81

INTELLIGENCE SUMMARY.

No. 64   Of HAZEBROUCK Sheet 1/100

Place	Date	Hour	Summary of Events and Information	Remarks and references to Appendices
AMES	Feb. 23		The Brigade resting & refitting. Equipment being overhauled. Guns were found to be in a bad condition. Breeches etc in good condition but sights & brackets require cleaning.	E.H.
AMES	July 24		Brigade resting & refitting	E.H.
AMES	Feb 25		" " 6/155 and wagons to J.A.17 workshops. 8/155 received spare parts for overhaul. At LABOURIERE for general overhaul.	E.H.
AMES	July 26		Orders were received for 32nd Divn Artillery. Officers, 1 mounted + 1 telephonist for battery & headquarters to be attached to Batteries & Headquarters of the 16th Divisional Artillery left group, for 4 days for the purpose of becoming acquainted with the enemy's front covered by 16 Division.	E.H.

INTELLIGENCE SUMMARY.

No 65

Of HAZEBROUCK sheet 1/10000

(Erase heading not required.)

Place	Date	Hour	Summary of Events and Information	Remarks and references to Appendices
AMES	July 27th		Parties for attachment to 16 Div. Artillery left HQrs 155 Bde RFA by Motor Bus at 5.40 am as under:—	
			H.Q. 2/Lieut R.F. ANGAS with 1 telephonist & 1 servant	
			A/155 2/Lieut W.W. NIMMO do do do	
			B/155 Lieut H. HIRST do do do	
			C/155 Major R.B. WARTON do do do	
			D/155 Capt. W.T. CALHAN do do do	
			Orders received for 2.18 pm & 1.2.15 How Batteries to be attached to	
			H.A. I Corps to act as "Counter Batteries"	
			A/155 C/155 D/155 men detailed for this work	
AMES	July 28		Lieut Col. P. SHEPPARD and other commanding A/155 C/155 & D/155 went to inspect the positions to be occupied by A.C.B. batteries as counter batteries	F.H.

INTELLIGENCE SUMMARY.

HAZEBROUCK 2nd [illegible] No 7/10/113
FRANCE Sheet 36 B 1/40,000

No. 66

Place	Date	Hour	Summary of Events and Information	Remarks and references to Appendices
AMES	July 28 (continued)		Orders received for 32nd Divl. Artillery to move to MARLES LES MINES & surrounding district. A.L.C. Batteries handed their pegging out parties g 10.1 14.4.1.6.5 Bthu.	Ett.
MARLES-LES-MINES	July 29		The 168th Brigade (1/n A/155, C/155 + D/155) marched from AMES to MARLES-LES-MINES via BELLERY-FERFAY-AUCHEL-LOZINGHEM. Brigade Headquarters established at the CHÂTEAU DE MARLES I 6.6.4.9. A/155, C/155 + D/155 marched to their wagon lines at L2.a.2.9, L13.d.2.9 + L13.c.6.5. while they went on to the W.A. I Corps for Lathies and anglecar. A/155 + C/155 drew their wagon lines of L2. 10.1. 16.4.1.6.8. B/155 retired but has returned from the Z.O.A. workshops at BETHUNE (guns) LABOURIERE (guns) + RUITZ (guns), in turn may take their wagon lines.	EM

INTELLIGENCE SUMMARY.

(Erase heading not required.) Rd FRANCE { Sht 36 B 1/40,000 { Sht 36 C 1/40,000

76 67

Place	Date	Hour	Summary of Events and Information	Remarks and references to Appendices
MARLES-LES-MINES	July 30th		Advance party of Officers & Other Ranks moved to Lesboeufs. H.Q. went to different headquarters to Dus Ritz. Position as under:- H.Q. Lt.Col. P.SHEPPARD D.S.O. B/155 CAPT V.HOLIDAY advance party returned from the 16" Divn Artly	EH
MARLES-LES-MINES	July 31st 1916		A.C. & D. Batteries in action in counter batteries at A/155 F.30. & a. 4.5 (about) with waggon lines at L.2a.3.9. B/155 G.27. c. 9.7 do. L.13.d.2.5. D/155 (how) M.16 (nr GRENAY CHURCH) L.13.c.6.6. Headquarters 155 Bde R.F.A. and B/155 at MARLES les MINES in rest and training	EH
</table>

Ebralstone Lt Col
Lt.-Colonel, R.F.A.
Commanding 155th Brigade, R.F.A.

32nd Divisional Artillery.

155th BRIGADE .R F. A.

AUGUST 1 9 1 6

WAR DIARY
or
INTELLIGENCE SUMMARY

Army Form C. 2118.

(Erase heading not required.)   MAR FRANCE Shut 36 B 1/40,000

No. 68

Instructions regarding War Diaries and Intelligence Summaries are contained in F. S. Regs., Part II. and the Staff Manual respectively. Title pages will be prepared in manuscript.

Place	Date	Hour	Summary of Events and Information	Remarks and references to Appendices
MARLE LES MINES	August 1st 1916	9 A	Orders received for all Battery commanders & officers to attend at 16 DH to move to Headquarters Left Group 3rd Div only to be attached to Battalion of 6th D.L.I. previous to relieving them. Lt Col P. SHEPPARD DSO. commanding 155 Bde R.F.A. returned to MARLE LES MINES.	EH
MARLE LES MINES	August 2nd 1916		LT. COL P. SHEPPARD DSO. 2/LIEUT ANGAS (orderly officer) 155 Bde R.F.A. with 6 Lieutenants (lieutenants from H.Q 155 Bde, Battery commanders & subalterns of 6 Stephenson & 6 M Lightbounds from A, B & D Batteries 155.3 H. R.F.A. moved to Headquarters 3rd D.H. Left Group. Batteries 9, 16 & 13th Bde R.F.A. are at work under 155 Bde R.F.A. to form part of the Left Group 32 D.A. Battery commanders & subalterns from 9 & 16 Stephenson's for posting, were attached to batteries of 3rd D.A.	EH

2353 Wt. W2544/1454 700,000 5/15 D.D.&L. A.D.S.S. Forms/C. 2118.

WAR DIARY
or
INTELLIGENCE SUMMARY.

Army Form C. 2118.

FRANCE Sheet 36 B 1/40000

No. 69

Place	Date	Hour	Summary of Events and Information	Remarks and references to Appendices
MARLE LES MINES	August 3rd 1916		Wagon lines selected for all batteries of the left group as under:- A/155 E2a39 B/155 9H&55 F7a65 D/155 F14352 B/164 F6b93 B/164 F6b93 C/164 F14b71 D/164 F14b52	EA
ANNEQUIN	August 4th 1916		Batteries moved to their new wagon lines as above near wagon lines before noon. Westmacker 155 Bde (left group) moved to F23d97. One section of each battery relieved section D.R.n D.A. after dark. A/155 & D/155 did not relieve between but moved their guns into emergency positions B/155 drew 2 guns from I.O.M availably & sent two in for overhaul.	EB

WAR DIARY or INTELLIGENCE SUMMARY

No. 70

Army Form C. 2118.

Place	Date	Hour	Summary of Events and Information	Remarks and references to Appendices
ANNEQUIN	April 5th 1916		Our action of batteries reported. The other spheres marked after dark. Ruts complete & Survey taken over by O.C. Light Group 32 DA (Lt Col P. SHEPPARD) at 10.50 a.m.	

Battery positions
O.P.

			Bearing (Mag)		Hor. L (yds)
A/155	G.7.b.90.15	A.21.a.25.10	30° – 70°		32° – 35°
B/155	F.24.c.83	do	72° – 90°		77° – 79½°
C/155	F.30.c.14				65° – 72°
A/124	F.24.c.65.55	A.20.d.9.7	50	110	90 – 95½°
B/164	F.30.a.30.65	A.20.d.10.33	80	117	96½ – 103½
C/164	F.29.a.25.33	B.20.d.70.15	78	139	77 – 85°
D/104	F.30.c.4.7	B.15.c.71.23	65	125	67 – 83°
		do	60	126	

GUNS in action A/155 – 4, B/155 – 2, B/124, 4, A/124, 4 B/160 – 2
C/164 – 4, D/164 – 4, Total 17 18pdr & 4.5" How.

Two guns of B/165 at J.O.A. working class from J. B/164

EJH

WAR DIARY
or
INTELLIGENCE SUMMARY.
(Erase heading not required.)

Place	Date	Hour	Summary of Events and Information	Remarks and references to Appendices
ANNEQUIN	AUGUST 6, 1916		All batteries registered on various points on the German line. Hostile artillery not very active. Enemy shelled Vermelles with A.A. guns: No. 77mm. + 15 10.5 cm shells. Hostile plane Kannen 8/11.45 (75) at 8.45 am & 1.10 pm but was driven off by our A.A. guns. Weather fine. Visibility good.	EH
ANNEQUIN	AUGUST 7, 1916		Working party at A.29.d.35.75. dispersed by our artillery. Hostile M.G. trailed at A.29.d.35.90. + fired on by 91.S.S. All batteries ordered systematically off 8.30pm our infantry ("sharps") throw a very A.A.21.d.65.05. Our artillery charged the enemy support line. communication trenches from 5.20 to 5.35. Enemy retaliated to the new may lights. Enemy machine gun & rifle fire was considerable during the night. Weather good. Wind South A.147, A.313. 3X259	EH

INTELLIGENCE SUMMARY.

Instructions regarding War Diaries and Intelligence Summaries are contained in F.S. Regs., Part II. and the Staff Manual respectively. Title pages will be prepared in manuscript.

Map 36c NE 1/20000
36c NW 1/10000

(Erase heading not required.)

Place	Date	Hour	Summary of Events and Information	Remarks and references to Appendices
ANNEQUIN	AUG 8 1916		Our artillery carried out some registration. Enemy artillery quiet. Weather good.	S.11
ANNEQUIN	Aug 9 1916		Very little artillery activity on either side. Some rifle fire & machine gun fire after dark. Weather bright & warm. Quiet.	S.11
~~ANNEQUIN~~ LE PREOL	Aug 10th 1916		Batt. Front Headquarters (SS R&) moved to LE PREOL. Batteries continued registering. Enemy shelled our R.E. & French Palissade Observation post	F.14 & 9.1 S.11
LE PREOL	Aug 11th 1916		We fired on enemy entrance at Quinchy Pair. He returned fire. enemy shelling our O.P.s near to trench on S. BRITISH FIRED A22c. On the whole the day was quiet. Bright moonlight night.	S.11

2353 Wt. W2544/1454 700,000 5/15 D. D. & L. A.D.S.S. Forms/C. 2115.

WAR DIARY
or
INTELLIGENCE SUMMARY.

Army Form C. 2118.

(Erase heading not required.)

Ref. 36ᵇNE 1/20000
36cNW 1/10000

Instructions regarding War Diaries and Intelligence Summaries are contained in F.S. Regs., Part II. and the Staff Manual respectively. Title pages will be prepared in manuscript.

Place	Date	Hour	Summary of Events and Information	Remarks and references to Appendices
LEPREOL	Aug 12		All batteries of the group continued registering. Enemy sent over 77 mm shells into our trenches to which we retaliated. 2/Lieut C.L. Paul A/155 transferred to C/164. Lieut J.F. Best C/164 transferred to A/155.	E.H.
LEPREOL	Aug 13		Our advance registered moved north behind the Somme line. Quiet day.	E.H.
LEPREOL	Aug 14		Everything quiet. Enemy & our artillery normal.	E.H.
LEPREOL	Aug 15		Some Trench Mortar activity. Front quiet. B/155 & HQ wagon lines moved to LE QUESNOY. F 86.66.	E.H.
LE PREOL	Aug 16		Artillery on this front normal. A/155 wagon lines moved to F 13 c 33	E.H.

INTELLIGENCE SUMMARY

36 B NE 1/20,000
36 C NW 1/20,000

(Erase heading not required.)

Place	Date	Hour	Summary of Events and Information	Remarks and references to Appendices
LE PREOL	August 17or18		No change, everything normal	F.9
LE PREOL	August 19		Enemy exploded a mine in A.2.b. No shelling activity of note	F.9
LE PREOL	-	20	A mine explosion was felt on our left flank followed by considerable shelling fire. All quiet on our front	F.9
LE PREOL	Aug	21 & 22	Front normal, no change	F.9
do		23	Situation normal, no change	F.9
do		24	H.Q. L.O.Y Group moved to F.16.a.3.6. Front quiet, weather good	F.9
do		25	No change, front normal	F.9

INTELLIGENCE SUMMARY

Army Corps: 75
Maps: 36 NE 1/20,000, 36 NW 1/20,000

Place	Date	Hour	Summary of Events and Information	Remarks and references to Appendices
LEPREOL.	Aug 26		During the night 25/26 no action. B/155 relieved 1 section C/164 1 section B/155 relieved 1 section B/155. Bn. ration C/164 took over from B/155 & took men and guns of relieved 2 battery section of 2 sections of the 16" Bomn. One section of B/164 relieved 1 section of 1 battery of 2 2 of 16" Bomn.	[sketch]
do	Aug 27"		During the night 26/27. Second section of B/155 relieved 2 "section" C/164 second section. B/155 relieved third section of B/155. C/164 took out ammunition of B/155 & relieved 1 section of battery of 2 sections of 16" Bomn. 2d section of B/164 relieved second section of 7.10 Bomn. Same road not manned from the morning of 27/8/16. d B/155 had one table over by railway beyond B/155. of 26 Bom only one complete lot been put out, and it to be shifted each day. B/155 came from under B/155 relieved ... relieved a battery of the 16" Bomn at G1ae.99	[sketch]

INTELLIGENCE SUMMARY.

(Erase heading not required.)

No. 76

Maps. 36 B NE 1/20000
36 C NW 1/20000

Place	Date	Hour	Summary of Events and Information	Remarks and references to Appendices
LE PREOL	Aug 28th		2/Lieut S.S. SEED B/155 and 2/Lieut H.M. TAYLOR D/155 were transferred to 1st Division. Lieut J.F. BEST A/155 transferred to B/155.	EH
LE PREOL	Aug 29th		Situation normal, no change. Heavy thunderstorm in the afternoon.	EH
LE PREOL	Aug 30		Weather wet, Situation had, front quiet.	
LE PREOL	Aug 31		Frost very quiet, weather fine, situation front.	

J. Clifford
Lt.-Colonel. R.F.A.
Comdg. 155th W. Y. Brigade, R.F.A.

32nd Divisional Artillery.

155th BRIGADE R. F. A.

SEPTEMBER 1 9 1 6

Army Form C. 2118.

WAR DIARY
or
INTELLIGENCE SUMMARY.

(Erase heading not required.) MAP Sheet 36 B NE
36 c NW

Instructions regarding War Diaries and Intelligence Summaries are contained in F. S. Regs., Part II. and the Staff Manual respectively. Title pages will be prepared in manuscript.

No 77

Place	Date	Hour	Summary of Events and Information	Remarks and references to Appendices
	1916			
LE PREOL	Sept 1		Enemy shelled BETHUNE to which we retaliated vigorously at 2.45 a.m. & at 5.15 a.m. Situation unchanged	EH
do	Sept 2		Situation normal. no change	EH
do	"	3.30	No change in the situation	EH
do	"	5	CAPT. V.NICHOLLS A/155 was transferred to 7th & 4th Army area 2/LIEUT W.W. MIMMO assumed command of A/155. Everything reported on this front	EH
do	"	67	Situation normal	EH
		8	LIEUT COL P.SHEPPARD D.S.O. (commanding 155 Bde R.F.A.) evacuated to ENGLAND. LT COL H. ALLCARD D.S.O. (commanding 154 Bde R.F.A.) assumed command of 155 Bde R.F.A.	EH

2353 Wt. W2544/1454 700,000 5/15 D. D. & L. A.D.S.S.Forms/C 2118.

WAR DIARY or INTELLIGENCE SUMMARY

Army Form C. 2118.

No. 78

(Erase heading not required.) Maps. Sheet 36 B N E 1/20,000
36 c NW

Place	Date	Hour	Summary of Events and Information	Remarks and references to Appendices
LE PREOL	Sept 9	6.14	Front very quiet. Very little activity on either side. Nothing occurred of any importance.	
	Sept 15		On the evening of the 15/16 position of C/155 moved to F24.c.8.3. overnight the two gun pits on the left of B/155. The Bgd a long engagement on a 6 gun basis B/155 with the left up (right gun) to B/155. to form a 6 gun battery. The other half goes to C/155 to form a 6 gun battery. Thus leaving the extent B/155, C/155, remain unchanged.	
	Sept 16		On the evening of 16/17, 2nd section C/155 moved to F.24.c.8.3. 1 gun B/155 moved from F24.c.8.3 to G.76.90.15. Disposition of B/155. evening at F24.c.8.3 with C/155 guns. The new battery (6 guns) B/155. The remaining B/155 engaged tonight became with the right gun B/155 which is actually at	

WAR DIARY or INTELLIGENCE SUMMARY

Army Form C. 2118

Instructions regarding War Diaries and Intelligence Summaries are contained in F. S. Regs., Part II. and the Staff Manual respectively. Title pages will be prepared in manuscript.

79

Place	Date	Hour	Summary of Events and Information	Remarks and references to Appendices
LEPREOL	16/9/16		G.y.k. 90.15 leaves the 3rd section of B/155.	
			LIEUT W.NIMMO remains in the new A/155	
			LIEUT G.J.ARMITAGE is transferred to D/155 from 2nd A/155	
			2/LIEUT J.W.TIPLADY is transferred to B/155 from 3rd A/165	
			CAPT. W.D WILKINSON is transferred to B/155 from late A/154	
			After the reorganisation the officers of the Brigade are as under	
			LIEUT COL. HALLCARD DSO. Commanding 155th Bde RFA	
			2/LIEUT E.Ford-Jones ADJUTANT	
			2/LIEUT R.F.ANGAS ORDERLY OFFICER	
			MAJOR R.B. WARTON Commanding A/155	
			LIEUT. C.P. DENBY, 2/LIEUT A.S.MERCER, 2/LIEUT G.M.PIAUD, 2/LIEUT W.W.NIMMO, 2/LIEUT K.F.FERGUSON (attached) } A/155	
			2/LIEUT G.J. ARMITAGE,	
			CAPT. V.HOLIDAY Commanding B/155	
			CAPT. W.D WILKINSON, LIEUT T.F. BEST, 2/LIEUT P.C. HUNT, 2/LIEUT E. LEET, 2/LIEUT J.W. TIPLADY } B/155	
			CAPT. W.J.CALMAN (commanding), LIEUT A. RHODES, 2/LIEUT J.H.LOCKYER } D/155	
			2/LIEUT A.J. DAVIS, 2/LIEUT H. HIRST, 2/LIEUT G.H.WIDGERY	

WAR DIARY
or
INTELLIGENCE SUMMARY.

(Erase heading not required.)

No 80

SHEET 36 c NW
MAP. SHEET 36 b NE } 1/20,000

Place	Date	Hour	Summary of Events and Information	Remarks and references to Appendices
LE PREOL	17.9.16		OLD C/155 wagon lines moved to wagon lines of OLD B/155 at F.13.a.9.2. Left section wagon line of OLD B/155 moved to B/155's wagon line at F.8.c.6.6. D/155 & 1 section (FERMELLES) B/155 came under R.E.George.	EA
LE PREOL	18.9.16		All gun teams delivered from 133 Bde & H.Q. 104 Bde transferred to 32nd D.A.C.	EA
LEPREOL	19.9.16 24.9.16		Nothing of importance to report	EA
"	24.9.16		Col. H.B. ALLEN late of 216 Bde R.F.A. joined this Brigade & was attached from this date.	EA
"	25.9/16 6.30/9/16		Front very quiet every thing normal and slack.	EA

H. Allen
Lt.Colonel, R.F.A.
Comdg. 155th W.Y. Brigade, R.F.A.

32nd Divisional Artillery.

155th BRIGADE R. F. A.

OCTOBER 1 9 1 6

WAR DIARY
or
INTELLIGENCE SUMMARY.

No. 81

M.A. Sect 36 NE 36 NW Vaccines

Place	Date	Hour	Summary of Events and Information	Remarks and references to Appendices
G.A 5" LE PREOL	4/5 Oct 1916		On the night of 4/5 Oct 1916 B/155 withdrawn from action at (F.24.2533) to its wagon line & became attached to 161 Bde	A

LE PREOL	6.A 10/1916		The 536th Battery (T.F.) on arrival at BETHUNE from ENGLAND was posted to 155 Bde R.F.A. & became B/155.
			
			Strength of battery:—
			Officers. Captain. H.A. Adams (T.F.)
			        Lieut N. Bark (T.F.)
			        Lieut E.S. Atkinson (T.F.)
			        Lieut E.P. Peel (T.F.)
			        Lieut J.F. Earle. S.R.
			
			O.Rs 134
			Horses 126
				B

Army Form C. 2118.

WAR DIARY
or
INTELLIGENCE SUMMARY.

(Erase heading not required.) *Mick Sheet* HAZEBROUCK Sheet 36 c N.W. 36 c N.E. 2000 1/10/1916

Place	Date	Hour	Summary of Events and Information	Remarks and references to Appendices
LE ROI	Oct 11th		A/155 , a section of C/168 and 1 section of D/168 came under the orders of the Right Group 5th Corp. D.A. 1 section C/168 , 1 section D/168 came under control of the Right Group 32 D.A. Headquarters 155 Bde. b ceased to be a Group Headquarters. C/155 (hoy) battery moved up into action at F.30.c.5.40.5. Waggon lines moved in at E.5.C. (BETHUNE) C/155 came under control of Right Group 32 D.A. 1/ for Ration	274
do	Oct 13		Capt. W.O. Wilkinson B/155 was struck off the strength of I Corps Brigade on being posted to R.E. 30 Division.	
do	Oct 15		Two sections A/155 & B/155 , 1 section C/155 , 1 bn section 2/155 moved out of action to their waggon lines after dark.	
LAPUGNOY	Oct 18		The whole of 155 Bde. marched to billets at LAPUGNOY in the afternoon "77L. 16". The section of batteries in action pulled out after dark & marched to LAPUGNOY E.P.	

2353 Wt. W2544/1454 700,000 5/15 D. D. & L. A.D.S.S.Forms/C. 2118.

WAR DIARY
or
INTELLIGENCE SUMMARY

Army Form C. 2118.

No 83   LENS Sheet 1/10,000 Shut 57 D 1/40,000

Place	Date	Hour	Summary of Events and Information	Remarks and references to Appendices
LATHIEULOY	Oct 17		155 Bde. marched to billets at LATHIEULOY with 20 cable section which was attached to the Brigade for the march South	E.A
REBREUVIETTE	Oct 18		155 Bde. and 20 cable section marched to billets at REBREUVIETTE	E.A
AUTHIEULE	Oct 19		155 Bde R.F.A. and 20 cable section marched to billets at AUTHIEULE. MAJOR R.B WARTON posted to 55th Divisional Artillery to take over duties of BRIGADE MAJOR. Capt POLLOCK (C/155) posted to 155 Bde R.F.A. to take command of A/155 vice MAJOR R B WARTON	E.A
MAILLY-MAILLET	Oct 20		155 Bde. R.F.A. marched to wagon lines & bivouacs at LOUVENCOURT. Headquarters 155 Bde. moved to MAILLY-MAILLET. A,B,C & D batteries moved up after dark into action as under:-	

Army Form C. 2118.

WAR DIARY
or
INTELLIGENCE SUMMARY.

(Erase heading not required.)

No 84 Sheet 57D 1/40000

Instructions regarding War Diaries and Intelligence Summaries are contained in F. S. Regs., Part II and the Staff Manual respectively. Title pages will be prepared in manuscript.

Place	Date	Hour	Summary of Events and Information	Remarks and references to Appendices
MAILLY-MAILLET	Oct 20 (contd)		A/155 at Q 4 a 3.7 B/155 at Q 4 a 5.5 C/155 at K 26 a 1.7 D/155 at Q 4 a 6.2 Headquarters, A, B, & D Batteries 155 Bde. come tactically under the 3rd Divn. Bty. 155 Bde. come tactically under O.C. 42nd Bde R.F.A.	EA
do	Oct 21		LIEUT A.V. RILEY on joining the Brigade is posted to B/155	EA
do	Oct 22		LIEUT W.G. BLACKIE on joining the Brigade is posted to B/155	EA
do	Oct 24		2/LIEUT A.J. DAVIES D/155 is posted to 22nd 99 Battery, I Corps	EA
do	Oct 28		C/155 Wagon Lines moved to ACHIEUX	
do	Oct 26 & 31		Nil.	

Y. A. Mearns

32nd Divisional Artillery.

155th BRIGADE/ R. F. A.

NOVEMBER 1 9 1 6

WAR DIARY
INTELLIGENCE SUMMARY

Army Form C. 2118.

No 85

Maj Shed 57 D/40000

Place	Date	Hour	Summary of Events and Information	Remarks and references to Appendices
MAILLY-MAILLET	Nov 3		A.B. & D. battery wagon lines moved to THIEVRES (1.14.A) 1/Lieut. P.C. HUNT (B/155) Transferred to 161 Bde R.F.A. T/Lieut. W.W. MIMMO (A/155) Transferred to B/155 as acting captain 2nd in command. LIEUT. RILEY B/155 Transferred to A/155	
do	Nov 4 "6.10"		A B & D batteries at "White City" (Q.4.a) were not firing. Batteries were heavily shelled intermittently.	
do	Nov 13		At 5.45 am attack on BEAUMONT-HAMEL SERRE at Y foreman lines from N.29 to R.20 commenced. 155 Bde cooperated. The chief task of the batteries at white city was to fire on my enemy restless observed moving. The day was very misty & the no. British were forced to return & return engine firmness commenced Trenches of enemy had two times inquired but not changed. (B battery) A man cart & 3 horses were blown up by a 4.50 c.m. shell	

WAR DIARY
or
INTELLIGENCE SUMMARY.

Maj 57 D

No 86

Place	Date	Hour	Summary of Events and Information	Remarks and references to Appendices
MAILLY - MAILLET	Nov 13		at the battery position when hanging up antenna. Casualties 2 O.Rs killed 4 O.Rs wounded Battery ever heavily shelled throughout the day and night	
	14		Operations continued A/155 had two men wounded and damaged. B/155 had 1 gun knocked out of action. Casualties - Capt W.T. Colman wounded D/155 wounded 1 O.R. wounded. Battery ordered to fire 1500 for teaching line Guns.	
			while Coy heavily shelled	
	15		Weather too bad to engage aeroplane targets firing on ordinary missions	
			gun sites	
	16		Operation good weather but much enemy activity. Battery B.H.F. very active shot on one A. D/155 ammunition pits Casualties 2 O.R's wounded A/4, one O.R.	

WAR DIARY or INTELLIGENCE SUMMARY

Army Form C. 2118.

No. 87

Month: Nov 57 D 1/40000

Place	Date	Hour	Summary of Events and Information	Remarks and references to Appendices
MAILLY-MAILLET	Nov	17	Situation quieter. Bright frosty day. Good observation. Relieved 1/5th on A/135. Riflemans dugout killed 1 OR + wounded two ORs.	A44
		18	Battery arrived in positions in attempt to take MUNICH TRENCH (Sheet. 57D SE & NE) Weather very wet and situation unsettled.	A44
		19	Quiet day. Batteries fired on German parties reported by aeroplane. Weather good + bright.	A44
		21	A, B and D batteries moved from "White City" to positions (camouflaged) at Q3a 8.9 Q3a 3.4 and Q3c 8.5 respectively.	A44
		22	ABND batteries registered on trenches from K 38 d 39 to K36c 1/2 7 1/2. K36c 1.5.	A44

Army Form C. 2118.

WAR DIARY
or
INTELLIGENCE SUMMARY.

No 88 Vol XI

(Erase heading not required.)

Place	Date	Hour	Summary of Events and Information	Remarks and references to Appendices
	24"		Group formed under Lieut Eleven consisting of 155, 161 & 126 Brigades & our 20" Infantry Brigade. Wound condition.	
	25"			
	30"		C/155 - Moved out of action to wagon line.	

J. Allentyre R.F.A.
Commdg 155 Brigade R.F.A.

32nd Divisional Artillery.

155th BRIGADE R. F. A.

DECEMBER, 1 9 1 6

WAR DIARY
or
INTELLIGENCE SUMMARY.

Army Form C. 2118.

Ref LENS Sheet 1/100000
SHEET 57 D 1/40,000

No 80.

4 JAN. 1917

Place	Date	Hour	Summary of Events and Information	Remarks and references to Appendices
LOUVENCOURT	Dec 4th		Batteries moved out of action to their wagon lines at THIEVRES	E.H.
ST LEGER	Dec 5	6	Hd qurs moved to LOUVENCOURT. The brigade marched into billets at ST LEGER	E.H.
ST LEGER	Dec 7th to Dec 31st		The brigade was at rest in billets. The time was spent in refitting training and in horse standings etc	E.H.

V H White Major RFA
commanding XV/63rd R.F.A

WAR DIARY

155th Bangalore RFA

Vol XIV (No. 90 & 95)

January 1st to January 31st 1917

Vol 13

* 1554 W.Y. BRIGADE, R.F.A. *
31 JAN 1917

WAR DIARY
INTELLIGENCE SUMMARY

Army Form C. 2118.

LENS 1/100,000
57 D 1/40,000

No 90

Place	Date	Hour	Summary of Events and Information	Remarks and references to Appendices
AUTHIEULE	Jan 2. 1917		The Brigade marched from our billets at St Leger to billets at AUTHIEULE	
MAILLY MAILLET.	Jan 3. 1917		Batteries moved into action as under. Wagon lines were established at LOUVENCOURT. Headquarters moved to MAILLY-MAILLET (Q7a23) – via DOULLENS. The Brigade came under the 7th Div Arty for tactical purposes & became the Right group 7th Div Arty. A B & D batteries became C group. 7th Div Arty. & battery is under the Right group 7th Div Arty. (22nd Bde RFA) BATTERY POSITIONS:- A/155 K.33 a 4.2. B/155 K.32 b 80.15 C/155 0.34 b 0.7 D/155 Q.2 a 9.3	
do	Jan 4. 1917		Wagon lines moved to between THIEVRES and AUTHIE. D/8 at I.14.b. D18 at I.9.c	

WAR DIARY
or
INTELLIGENCE SUMMARY.
(Erase heading not required.)

Army Form C. 2118.

No 91

570. N40000
570 SE Y43000

Place	Date	Hour	Summary of Events and Information	Remarks and references to Appendices
MAILLY-MAILLET	Jan 5. 1917		C group is in support of the Left Group of "D" Div Arty & covers the same front. Batteries selected supporting in preparation for forthcoming operations (the taking of MUNICH TRENCH) in accordance with 7"Div Arty. O.O. No 63.	
do	Jan 10th		Two new officers joined the brigade from ENGLAND and were posted to batteries as follows. LIEUT. D. NATHAN to B/155", 2/LIEUT A.R. BARNES to B/155" 2/LIEUT W.G. BLACKIE (B/155) struck off the strength of the brigade (Medical board unfit on leaving)	
do	Jan 11th		The Brigade took part in minor operations which were successful in taking MUNICH TRENCH	
do	Jan 14		Orders were received for the 32nd Div Arty. to relieve the 3rd Div Arty. The relief of batteries to take place section by section on the nights of the 16/17" & 17/18" & the ammunition on the nights 17/18	
do	Jan 15		Battery Commanders reconnoitred their new positions prior to relieving the 3rd Div Arty. Relief to take place as follows A/155 to relieve 107 Bde R.F.A. B/155 to relieve 108th Bde R.F.A. D/155 to relieve D/23 R.F.A. C/155 did not relieve their card had not to their arrival late.	

Army Form C. 2118.

WAR DIARY
or
INTELLIGENCE SUMMARY.
(Erase heading not required.)

No 92

Instructions regarding War Diaries and Intelligence Summaries are contained in F. S. Regs., Part II. and the Staff Manual respectively. Title pages will be prepared in manuscript.

Map Sheet 57D 1/40000
"HEBUTERNE" 57D NE 3rd parts 1/10000

Place	Date	Hour	Summary of Events and Information	Remarks and references to Appendices
MAILLY - MAILLET	Jan 16.1917		2LIEUT G.D. BOTTOMLEY (C/155) invalided sick to ENGLAND, contribute of the Stoff of the Brigade. One section of A.B.& D. batteries relieves one section of 107, 108 & D/23 batteries respectively. One section C/155 with draw to its wagon line.	M/1 G.B.
COURCELLES	Jan 17.1917		The remaining sections of A.B.&D. batteries relieved sections of 107,108 & D/23 batteries respectively. Remaining section of C/155 withdraw to its wagon line. Headquarters 156 Bde. moved to COURCELLES, relieved HQrs 23rd Bde. Batteries occupied position as under:-	
			Battery — Battery position — O.P. — Front covered	
			A/155 — K27a 1.5¾ — K27b19 — K3d7 2.2 - K23b 7.0	
			B/155 — K20d 6.5 — K21d 3¾.7¾ — K23b 7.0 - K23b1.7	
			C/155 — K20d 2.0 — K21d ¾.8 — K23d 7.2.2 - K23b1.27	
			Lieut J Lombard (T.F.) in command the Brigade was posted to A/155	
			Lieut R Lowden (S.R.) — do — B/155	
			Lieut A Campbell (T.C.) — do — B/155	
			Lieut R.M. Lyttleton (T.C.) — do — D/155	G/1

Army Form C. 2118.

WAR DIARY
or
INTELLIGENCE SUMMARY.
(Erase heading not required.)

Map sheet 1/40,000 57D
HEBUTERNE sheet 1/10,000

Instructions regarding War Diaries and Intelligence Summaries are contained in F.S. Regs., Part II. and the Staff Manual respectively. Title pages will be prepared in manuscript.

No 93

Place	Date	Hour	Summary of Events and Information	Remarks and references to Appendices
COURCELLES	Jan 18th	—	The front covered by 155 Bde is taken over by the 19th Division. A, B & D batteries 155 Bde come under the control of the R/H Group 19th Div Arty for tactical. 2 Officers and 22 O.R. per battery from A, B & D batteries 311 Bde 62nd Div are attached respectively to A/155, B/155 & D/155 for instructional purposes. The officers of 311 Bde (77) and 8 O.R. are attached to Headquarters 155 Bde (77)	ZH
COURCELLES	Jan 20th		C/155 is split up. The right section is posted to D/151 Bde & the left section to D/168 Bde. Lieut N Back & Lieut Pret reports to D/168 Lieut Robinson is posted to D/161 Lieut G F Earle is posted to D/155 Capt V H F Newcome is attached to D/155	ZH

2353 Wt. W2544/1454 700,000 5/15 D. D. & L. A.D.S.S. Forms/C. 2118.

WAR DIARY or INTELLIGENCE SUMMARY

Army Form C. 2118

No 94

Map Sheet 57D 1/40,000
HEBUTERNE Sheet 1/10,000

Place	Date	Hour	Summary of Events and Information	Remarks and references to Appendices
COURCELLES	Jan 25		The left section of the 517" How Battery (2/169) marched to D/155. Strength of section 2 Officers 1/Lieut F Buckham 2/Lieut D H Marsden O.R. 58 horses 44 Guns & Limbers 2 (4.5 how) Ammunition Wagons (4.5 how) 4	EM
COURCELLES	Jan 26	9	The newly joined section of D/155 moved up into action at A20a92	EM
do	Jan 29		Two G.S. wagons & 4.5 How Ammunition Wagons, 12 drivers, 12 L.D. horses, 9 mules joined the 155th Bde. from the 31st D.A.C. This detail will form part of the Brigade ammunition column shortly to be formed every to 155 Bde forming an Army Field Artillery Brigade. This detail is attached to D/155 until the B.A.C. is formed.	EM

Army Form C. 2118

WAR DIARY
or
INTELLIGENCE SUMMARY
(Erase heading not required.)

No 95

Place	Date	Hour	Summary of Events and Information	Remarks and references to Appendices
COURCELLES	Jan 31st		A portion of the 32nd D.A.C. was taken over by 155 Bde. to form the 155" B.A.C. under Captain WORREL. The detail from the 31st D.A.C. which was attached to D/155" B.A.C. is posted to 155" B.A.C. The 155" B.A.C. will be brought up to strength at a later date by details from the 61st D.A.C.	A/1

H. Alcock
Lieut Col. R.F.A.
Commanding, 155 Bde, R.F.A.

WAR DIARY.
155th (ARMY) F.A. Bde.

VOL XV (No. 96 to 99)

February 1st to February 28th, 1917

WAR DIARY or INTELLIGENCE SUMMARY

Army Form C. 2118

No 9 ?

Place	Date	Hour	Summary of Events and Information	Remarks and references to Appendices
COURCELLES	Feb 1st 1917		Lieut F BAREHAM (D/155) is posted to 155" B.A.C.	61
COURCELLES	Feb 10"		The late A/306 Battery 61st Div. joined 155 Brigade & became C/155 battery. C/155 is billeted at ORVILLE. Strength of Battery on arrival :- Officers 5 — Major H.D. DAY, Capt. G.S. JAMES, 2/Lieut St DICKINSON, 2/Lieut F L, 2/Lieut M D SCOTT O.R.s 191 Horses 137 18 pdr guns 6 18 pdr ammn 12 Motorcycle 1 Watercart 1 G.S. Wagons 2 (Tech) Bicycles 6 5 G.S.O.R.s, 15 L.D. horses, 8 3 mules 6 18 pdr Wagons 2, 4.5 How Wagons 2 G.S. wagons joined this brigade from the 61st D.A.C. & were posted to 155" B.A.C. G.J. ARMITAGE (A/155) 2/Lieut on being attached to the R.F.C. is struck off the strength of the brigade.	112

Army Form C. 2118

WAR DIARY
or
INTELLIGENCE SUMMARY
(Erase heading not required.)

No 98

Map 1/40000 Sheet 57D
1/10000 TRENCH MAP HEBUTERNE

Place	Date	Hour	Summary of Events and Information	Remarks and references to Appendices
COURCELLES	Feb 18		Right Artillery Group 19th Div. A reorganised in accordance with Right Group O.O. No 3 attached. Lieut R.E. FERGUSON (A/155) on being posted to "R" A.A Battery is struck off the strength of the Brigade	EA
COURCELLES	" 19		A/155 & B/155 pass to the control of CENTRE GROUP 19th Divl Artly in accordance with RIGHT GROUP O.O. No 4 attached.	EA
do	" 20		A/86, B/86, D/86 moved into positions at K33c32; K27a19; & K26b96 respectively & are attached to RIGHT GROUP for defensive purposes only. These batteries are not to be called on except in an extreme emergency.	EA
do	" 21		Batteries of 86 Bde come under control of O.C. E6 Bde. All batteries of 155 Bde. come under control of O.C. 155 Bde.	EA

WAR DIARY
or
INTELLIGENCE SUMMARY

(Erase heading not required.)

Army Form C. 2118

No 77

Place	Date	Hour	Summary of Events and Information	Remarks and references to Appendices
COURCELLES	Feb 27		Conquest on the attacked by the enemy. 155 Bde batteries moved forward into position in K29d.	
			A battery at K29d 84	
			B " " K29d 73	
			C " " K29d 42	
			D " " K29d 10	
			OP for all batteries at K30a 7.4	
			F.O.O. at Bde HQ at K24b 8062	E11

J.P. Allcock
Lieut. Col. RFA
Commanding 155 (Army) F.A. Bde.

W.G.R.By.   Copy No. 14

Right Artillery Group Operation Order No.1.

Reference REGINTRENCH SHEET 1/10,000.

1. On the withdrawal of the 32nd.Divisional Artillery from the line on the nights 16th/17th and 17th/18th inst., the Right Group will be re-organised as follows:-

    Commander: Lieut-Colonel. E.Allgood,D.S.O.
    Headquarters 155th (ARMY) R.A. Brigade.
    18 Prs.   A/155 Battery.
               B/155 Battery.
               C/155 Battery.
               D/86 Battery.
    4.5"Hows. D/155 Battery.

2. A, B, & D batteries 155th Brigade,R.F.A. will remain as at present.
    C/155 will take over from C/160.
    C/86 will take over from C/161.

3. Battery positions, Zones of fire, S.O.S. lines, O.P's etc., are shown in Appendix "A" attached.

4. Ammunition.

    Batteries of the Right Group will take over ammunition from batteries of the 32nd.Div.Arty., as follows:-

    C/155 from   { C/160 at K.27.c.2.7.
                 { A/160 at K.26.a.1.6.

    C/86 from   { C/161 at K.27.c.3.2.
                 { B/160 at K.26.a.0.4.

    On completion of reliefs Battery Commanders will report amounts of ammunition taken over.

5. Intelligence.

    O.P's, Maps, Photographs, S.O.S.Orders, Retaliation Schemes, Diagram of communications, and all information relating to the Zone covered will be taken over from batteries relieved.
    C/86 will take over the above Intelligence from B/160 and C/160.   C/86 will take over Intelligence from C/155 at K.27.a.85.55.

6. Liaison with the Infantry.

    A, B, and C/155 batteries will cover the Left Battalion in L.A.P. Sec or and the present Liaison arrangements will hold.
    C/155, C/86, and D/86 will cover the Right Battalion in L.C.Sector.
    C/155, and C/86 will find a Liaison Officer to live at Battn. Headquarters alternately. C/155 doing the first tour of duty on completion of reliefs.
    Length of tour of duty and times of relief of Liaison Officers will be arranged between O.C.Batteries and Battn.Commanders.

APPENDIX "A"

Battery Position.	O.P.	Max. Arcs.	Normal Arcs.
B/155 K.20.d.68.46	K.21.d.07.77	68deg.– 108deg.	78deg.– 88deg.
A/155 K.27.a.1.4	K.27.b.1.8	66 ,, – 105 ,,	76 ,, – 86 ,,
C/86 K.27.c.32.27	(K.21.d.4.4 (K.33.b.6.6	61 ,, – 107 ,,	73 ,, – 81 ,,
C/155 K.27.c.3.2	K.27.d.8.0	67 ,, – 107 ,,	87 ,, – 98 ,,
D/155 K.26.a.2.9	K.21.d.07.80	58 ,, – 122 ,,	76 ,, – 105 ,,
~~D/86 K.33.a.3.2.~~	~~K.21.c.9.0~~	~~?~~	~~63 ,, – 80 ,,~~

S.O.S. Lines.

B/155 K.23.b.35.60., K.23.b.43.45., K.23.b.53.30., K.23.b.53.12., K.23.d.60.95., K.23.d.70.85.

A/155 K.23.d.80.70., K.23.d.72.56., K.23.d.70.40., K.23.d.70.25., K.23.d.63.07., K.29.b.57.92.

C/86 K.29.b.50.75., K.29.b.36.63., K.29.b.30.45., K.29.b.20.30., K.29.b.1215., K.29.d.05.97.

C/155 K.29.d.05.80., K.29.d.12.65., K.29.d.15.50., K.29.d.05.30., K.29.d.10.20., K.29.d.10.05.,

D/155 K.~~23.b.0.7.~~, K.23.b.7.6., ~~K.23.b.95.50.~~, K.24.a.1.1., K.24.c.1.4., ~~K.23.d.95.20.~~

~~D/86~~ ~~K.29.b.10.90.~~, K.29.b.95.65., ~~K.29.b.60.40.~~, K.29.b.70.00., K.29.d.40.45., ~~K.29.d.60.30.~~

FRONT COVERED.

Batteries.			
B/155	Left Boundary.	K.23.b.4.6)	EASTWARDS.
	Right Boundary.	K.23.d.85.75)	
A/155	Left Boundary.	K.23.d.85.75)	EASTWARDS.
	Right Boundary.	K.29.b.6.8)	
C/86	Left Boundary.	K.29.b.6.8)	EASTWARDS.
	Right Boundary.	K.29.d.10.95)	
C/155	Left Boundary.	K.29.d.10.95)	EASTWARDS.
	Right Boundary.	K.29.d.20.00)	
D/155	Left Boundary.	K.23.b.4.6	
	Right Boundary.	~~K.29.d.6.8~~ 29 d 2000	,,
~~D/86~~	~~Left Boundary.~~	~~K.29.b.6.8~~	,,
	~~Right Boundary.~~	~~K.29.d.20.00~~	

SECRET.   COPY No. 14

AMENDMENT to NIGHT ARTILLERY GROUP O.O.No.5.

Para 1. line 11. Delete B/86 Battery.

Para 2. line 9. Delete B/86 will occupy a position at C.33.a.3.2

Para 5. Before leaving their positions A., B., & D/106 will hand
over Battery boards, Aeroplane photographs, and Secret
maps to Group Headquarters, and not as previously stated.
Retaliation Schemes, S.O.S.orders, and information regarding
the Zone will be handed over as follows :-

   A/106 and B/106 to C/86.

   D/106 ... ... to B/151.

APPENDIX "A"., line 3., delete 60deg.-92deg. and substitute
60deg - 100deg.

line 6., delete 91deg., and substitute 101deg.

line 9., delete D/86 K.33.a.3.2.   K.21.a.9.0. 7. 63deg 60deg.

lines 19 and 20., delete K.23.b.6.7., K.23.b.9030., K.23.d.9320.,
and substitute, K.29.b.95.63., K.29.b.70.00., K.29.d.40.95.

line 21., delete D/86   K.30.a.10.90., K.29.b.95.63.,
K.29.b.60.40., K.29.d.70.00., K.29.d.40.95., K.29.d.60.10.

line 34., delete K.29.b.6.4 and substitute K.29.d.20.00.

Delete lines 35 and 36.

                                              [signature]
                                              Lieut. R.F.A.
14/3/17.   Adjutant, Night Artillery Group, 19th Div.

War Diary
9

SECRET.   Copy No. ....9....

NIGHT ARTILLERY GROUP OPERATION ORDER No. 4.
───

1. The 58th Infantry Brigade will relieve the 57th Infantry Brigade
    in H.1.Sector to-night 17/18th Feby.

2. In order to adapt the organisation of the artillery Brigade
    of the 19th Divisional Front to the above change, the NIGHT
    Artillery Group will take over from the RIGHT ARTILLERY GROUP
    A/153 and B/153.

3. The dividing point of the zones of responsibility of the RIGHT
    and CENTRE ARTILLERY GROUPS will be K.23.c.65.60.

4. The above change will necessitate a change in the S.O.S. lines
    for B/153 and C/86.
    No other alterations will be necessary for batteries of the
    NIGHT ARTILLERY GROUP.

5. New S.O.S. lines for B/153 and C/86 will be :-

        B/153.   K.9?.d.12.89., K.29.d.68.41., K.29.d.42.47.,
                  K.29.d.45.65., K.29.d.65.80., K.29.d.63.10.

        C/86.   K.29.d.15.93., K.29.d.30.75., K.29.d.30.55.,
                  K.29.d.25.40., K.29.d.12.20., K.29.d.05.97.

6. Time at which above changes will take place will be notified
    later.

7. ACKNOWLEDGE.

                                            [signature]
                                                    Lieut.,R.F.A.,
16.2.17.   Adjutant NIGHT ARTILLERY GROUP 19th Div.

Copy No. 1. A/153.
        2. B/153.
        3. C/153.
        4. D/153.
        5. 58th.Infantry.
        6. War Diary.
        9. War Diary.